OPTIONS TRADING
CRASH COURSE

THE MOST COMPLETE GUIDE THAT WILL SHOW YOU HOW TO MAKE MONEY
TRADING WITH OPTIONS. BECOME AN EXPERT TRADER WITH BEGINNER AND
ADVANCED STRATEGIES TO EARN
PASSIVE INCOME

ARTHUR D. RICHIE

Table of Contents

Introduction

Financial Freedom

Many people seek it, but few have it. That is because the secrets behind obtaining it are closely guarded by those who have it. This book is about exposing one true and reliable way that you can earn the financial security and independence you need to control the way you live your daily life.

Signs of Financial Slavery

The first active step needed to get started on a financial freedom journey is acknowledging that you are not financially stable or free. This pill is hard to swallow for some people and so, they avoid acknowledging it even with the overwhelming evidence to support the state.

Facing this fact is not about demeaning your integrity or bring you down. It is about giving you a foundation to start with to build the financial security you need. This knowledge is needed to show you where you currently stand financially and your resources to develop a plan to get where you need and want to be.

The following conditions are those that chain many people to financial slavery:

- **Living paycheck to paycheck:** People who live this way do not have an emergency fund and typically have accompanying credit card debt because they need to subsidize their expenses higher than their income. Many people live this way. More than 40% of American households could not cover a $400 expense such as medical bills or car repairs if it came up unexpectedly in 2017.

- **Not having enough saved up to sustain their lifestyle if they were to lose their job:** People such as these do not have enough money accumulated to take time away from working daily. That's why most people are in careers and jobs that bring them no joy. They need the salary to keep a roof over their heads and food in their belly, and so, they deal with the circumstances that make them unhappy.

- **Not being able to pursue the activities and adventures that bring happiness while still saving and accumulating wealth:** These types of people are stuck in a cycle of trading their daily hours for money. They still cannot enjoy the money they earn because it is not enough to pay the bills.

- **Having inflexible schedules:** Most people are stuck in a cycle of working every day and going home to come back to work the next day. They have to give this time to earn an income they want and become chained to their jobs.

- **Not being able to retire comfortably at the desired age:** The world over, the average age for retirement is 65 years old. However, many people are not expected to live even 20 years past that age. That does not live much time to enjoy a life free of accumulating all the wealth you need. The sadder fact is most people do not retire with enough money saved up to enjoy the things that they want after retirement. Some others still have to work a job even after this age to sustain themselves. Financially free people can retire at the age they want rather than be dictated by someone else. They also have the capital available to do the things they want to do and still have income coming to them on a more passive basis.

- **Spend more money than earned:** This results because people want to live the lifestyle that they want but cannot afford, or people needing to subsidize their income to cater to their needs. To build wealth, you cannot have more money going out than coming in. Signs that your income exceeds your spending include, for instance, having a budget based on your salary, having an expense list that exceeds your net income, carrying a balance on your credit card, having rent or mortgage that is more than 30% of your net income and buying things to impress or keep up with other people.

Are you slave to your finances? Would you like to use your time in other ways while still earning a steady and growing income? Can you use an extra income to develop the lifestyle you want?

If your answer is yes to any of these income questions, or relating to even just one of the conditions stated above, means you can use the advice and strategies outlined in this book.

What Financial Freedom Is and Why Only a Few People Have It

Having financial freedom is more than just having a 6-month emergency fund saved up and your debt cleared. Financial freedom means taking control of your time and finances to do what you want to do rather than what your bank account figure dictates—being financially free means you do not need to trade your time for money.

To be able to gain this financial freedom, you need to have financial security. Financial security is the condition whereby you support the standard of living you want now and in the future by having stable income sources and other available resources. That means not living paycheck to paycheck. It means not having to worry about where your next dollar is coming from. It means having a huge weight lifted off your shoulders because you know there are resources you can leverage to get the things that you want and need.

People who have financial freedom are also financially independent. Financial independence is the state of having personal wealth to maintain the lifestyle and the standard of living you want without having to trade your daily hours for money. The assets and resources you have generated will gain that income for you so that your income remains far greater than your expenses. In essence, being financially independent means, you can go for a prolonged period without trading time for money and still have the standard of living that you want. You can go on a year-long vacation and still be secure knowing that your wealth is still growing.

To be financially independent, you must have:

- An emergency fund that can sustain your lifestyle for an extended period (maybe even years)
- Assets that produce income for you on a daily, weekly, monthly, and yearly basis
- Very little or zero debt.

Very few people on the planet are financially secure and independent. More than 1 billion people live in extreme poverty. In 2015, it was estimated that more than 10% of the global population lived on less than US$1.90 per day.

Despite these statistics, there is hope. This hope comes from the fact that this statistic goes down every year. In fact, in 2019, less than 8% of the global population lived in extreme poverty. This fact is largely attributed to the condition that people are more educated about their options and do not accept these poor circumstances.

Despite this improvement, most of the global population still trades their time for an hourly wage. The income earned from this is not sustainable, nor will it allow these people to live the standard of life they would like. They will not be able to retire comfortably. There is no power or security in living this way.

Financially free people have learned and harnessed the power of passive income. Passive income is generated from little to no effort or earned to exchange time for money over the long term. While it might take a massive amount of time and effort to establish in the beginning, passive income allows you to earn money even while you sleep, with little to no daily effort required for its maintenance.

The beauty of passive income is that it is limited to one income bracket or a portion of the population. Anyone can develop passive income as long as these people develop the right mindset and are willing to put in the time and effort to learn and be consistent in pursuing this standard of living.

Habits and Mindset of the Financially Free

I state the habits and the mindset needed for financially free persons in this part because no matter how effective the strategies I will outline in the rest of this book, they will be useless unless the practitioner molds his or her mind to be consistent and persistent. You cannot be on and off again with the strategies that you implement to gain financial freedom.

You have to eliminate the limiting belief that what you are currently is all you can ever be. You would better have a mindset that promotes growth. Your mindset is your frame of mind: the things that you believe, your thoughts, and your opinions. Your education thus far, your upbringing, your religion, and many other things shape your mindset. Thus, your mindset determines how you perceived the outside world, yourself, and what you can achieve.

Your attitude is a manifestation of your mindset, and it shows whether your mindset is limiting you or helping you grow. A growth mindset encourages making extra time and effort to grow intelligence and experience to make a better living standard. On the other hand, a fixed mindset is one where it is believed that all our qualities are fixed, and born talent is the only fact determining success. This type of mindset limits a person's capacity for learning, while a growth mindset is one where there is no limit to potential or success.

You need to develop a growth mindset to move from your current financial position to one where you are financially free. The characteristics of someone who has a growth mindset include:

- Talent and intelligence can be developed through effort and learning.
- Mistakes are a part of learning, and that failure is an opportunity for learning and growth.
- Failure is a temporary setback and not permanent feedback to ability and talent.
- Embrace challenges and change as opportunities.
- Receive constructive feedback openly from other people to further develop your learning process.
- View constructive feedback as a valuable resource of information.
- View the success of other people as a source of information and inspiration.

By opening your mind and imagining the possibilities, you can find fulfillment in not just your financial life but in your life as an entirety.

Developing a growth mindset is not innately ingrained in every human being. It is something that you have to work on, and the best way to do so is to develop habits that will encourage you to think differently and adaptively. Such habits include:

- **Developing your mission statement:** Success is a personal and individualized process. Therefore, if you would like to be financially free, you have to know how this is meaningful to you and what financial success means to you on an individual basis.

- **Being goal-oriented:** You need to be clear on what you want out from your future and then work diligently in your effort to earn it.

- **Continually learning and seeking new experiences:** This allows you to broaden your horizons and gain more experiences to shape your mind into forward-thinking.

CHAPTER 1:

The Basics in Options Trading

Option contracts usually refer to the purchase or sale of certain assets. An option is a contract between two parties (a buyer and a seller), in which whoever buys the option acquires the right to exercise what the agreement indicates, although he will not have an obligation to do so.

Option contracts commonly refer to purchasing or selling certain assets, stocks, stock indices, bonds, or others. These contracts also establish that the operation must be carried out on a pre-established date (in the European ones, since those of the U.S. are exercised at any time) and at a fixed price when the contract is signed.

It is necessary to make an initial disbursement to purchase an option to buy or sell (called "premium"). Its value depends, fundamentally, on the market asset price, the variability of that price, and the period between the contract's date and its expiry date.

Call and Put

The options that grant the right to buy are called "Call," and the options that grant the right to sell are called "Put." Additionally, they are called European options that can only be exercised on the date of exercise; American Options can be used during the contract's life.

When the time comes for the buying party to exercise the option, if it does, two situations occur:

Whoever appears as the seller of the option will be obliged to do what the said contract indicates: sell or buy the asset to the counterparty if it decides to exercise its right to buy or sell.

Who appears as the option buyer will have the right to buy or sell the asset. However, if it doesn't suit you, you can refrain from making the transaction.

An option contract usually contains the following specifications:

- **Exercise date:** The expiration date of the right is included in the option.
- **Exercise price:** The agreed price for the asset's purchase/sale referred to in the contract (called an underlying asset).

- **Option premium or price**: The amount paid to the counterparty to acquire the right to buy or sell.
- **Rights acquired with the purchase of an option:** They can be Call (the right of purchase) and Put (the right of sale).
- **Types of Option:** There may be Europeans, only exercised on the date that you can exercise it, or American, to be used at any time during the contract. There are, besides, other more complex types of options, the so-called "Exotic Options."

In international financial markets, the types of options that are traded on organized exchanges are typically American and European.

Practical Example

Purchase of a Call option by an importing company to secure the Euro price on that day.

To better understand the use of options, this example is presented by an importing company that wants to ensure against increases in the Euro's price.

To do so, you can buy a European Call option today that gives you the right to buy a million euros, within three months, at $ 550 per Euro. To acquire that right, the company pays $ 2 per Euro; that is, the option premium has a cost of $ 2,000,000.

If on the expiration date of the option, the price of the Euro in the market is over $ 550 (for example, at $ 560), the company will exercise the option to buy them, as it will only pay $ 550 per Euro.

On the contrary, if on that date the market price of the Euro was below $ 550 (for example at $ 530), the company will not exercise the option since it makes no sense to pay $ 550 per Euro when it can be purchased at the market at $ 530; in this case, the option expires without being exercised.

The cash flows are as follows:

Today (April 10, 20XX).

Buy a European Call option, which gives you the right to buy USD 1,000,000 to $ 550 on October 10, 20XX, as the value of the premium is 2 and 1,000,000 contracts are purchased (which means that the notional of the agreement is the U.S. $ 1) there is a cash outlay of $ 2,000,000 for that concept.

Expiration date (October 30, 20XX)

If the Euro is above the option's exercise price, it would be exercised, and $ 550 per Euro will be paid, that is, $ 550,000,000.

Otherwise, the option expires if it is used, and the euros are acquired in the market. The euros purchased are used to cancel the importation of goods or services.

The following table shows the result of the operation. As can be seen, if on the expiration date of the option contract, the market exchange rate is lower than the exercise price of the Call option, the importer will end up paying the market price per Euro plus the cost of the premium; otherwise, the cost of each Euro will be equal to the exercise price plus the premium. In strict rigor, the premium value should be updated for the interest that would have been earned if that money had been deposited instead of paying the value of the premium. That is, the importer will have made sure to pay a maximum of $ 552 per Euro.

Market exchange rate A	The exercise price of the option B	Premium C	Value of the options (1) $D = (A - B)$	Result of the options (2) $E = D - C$	Disbursement for purchase of euros (3) F	Total disbursement $G = F + C$
530	550	2,000,000	0	-2,000,000	530,000,000	532,000,000
540	550	2,000,000	0	-2,000,000	540,000,000	542,000,000
550	550	2,000,000	0	-2,000,000	550,000,000	552,000,000
560	550	2,000,000	10,000,000	8,000,000	550,000,000	552,000,000
570	550	2,000,000	20,000,000	18,000,000	550,000,000	552,000,000
580	550	2,000,000	30,000,000	28,000,000	550,000,000	552,000,000

Notes:

1. On the expiration date, when the price of the Euro in the market is lower than the exercise price, the value of the Call option will be zero (as it is not appropriate to exercise the purchase right), whereas, if the opposite occurs, the value of the Call option will correspond to the difference between those two prices.
2. That result represents how much money was paid or saved by the fact of coverage.
3. Currencies are acquired when it is not optimal to exercise the option or exercise the right of purchase when exercising that right is an optimal decision.

Finally, it should be noted that if a forward-type contract with the same delivery price had been used to perform the same coverage, the importer would have ended up always paying $ 550. However, it would not have had the opportunities (which may appear when hedging with Call options) to benefit from declines in the market exchange rate. Also, note that the operation is much simpler to perform: a premium is paid at the time of purchasing the option and on the expiration date (or at any time before that date if the options were of the American type) at least the price that has been agreed.

How the Options Work

Options operators must understand the complexity that surrounds them. Knowing the options' operation allows operators to make the right decisions and offers them more options when executing a transaction.

Indicators:

- The value of an option consists of several elements that go hand in hand with the "Greeks."

- The price of the guaranteed value

- Expiration

- Implied volatility

- The actual exercise prices

- Dividends

- Interest rates

The "Greeks" provide valuable information on risk management and rebalance portfolios to achieve the desired exposure (e.g., Delta coverage). Each Greek measures the reaction of the portfolios to small changes in an underlying factor, which allows the individual risks to be examined:

- The Delta measures the rate of change of the value of an option regarding changes in the underlying asset price.

- The Gamma measures the change rate in the Delta with the changes suffered by the underlying asset price.

- Lambda or elasticity refers to the percentage change in the value of an option compared to the percentage change in the price of the underlying asset, which offers a method of calculating leverage, also known as "indebtedness."

- Theta calculates the option value's sensitivity over time, a factor known as "temporary wear."

- Vega measures the susceptibility of the option of volatility. Vega measures the value of the option based on the volatility of the underlying asset.

- Rho represents the sensitivity of the value of an option against variations in the interest rate and measures the option's value based on the risk-free interest rate.

Therefore, the Greeks are reasonably simple to determine if the Black Scholes model (considered the standard option valuation model) is used and is very useful for intraday and derivatives traders. Delta, Theta, and Vega are useful tools to measure time, price, and volatility. The value of the option is directly affected by maturity and volatility if:

- For a long period before expiration, the value of the purchase and sale option tends to rise. The opposite situation will occur if the value of the purchase and sale options is prone to a fall for a short period before expiration.

- If the volatility increases, so will the value of the purchase and sale options, while if the volatility decreases, the value of the purchase and sale options decreases.

- The guaranteed value price causes a different effect on the purchase options' value than on the sale options.

- Usually, as the securities price increases, so do the current purchase options that correspond to it, increasing its value while the sale options lose value.

- If the price of the value falls, the opposite happens, and the current purchase options usually experience a drop in value while the value of the sale options increases.

CHAPTER 2:

The Pros and Cons of Options Trading

This aspect is one of the most common questions by people. Why do you want to exchange options?

Well, the first reason for this is to protect and control your risk. If you take a big risk, trading options is the way to protect yourself so that you don't lose all your money. It gives you full control of how and where your money is going. But one thing you should know is that trading options should not be done with your eyes closed. You're going to have to keep an eye on the market. And if you don't, it's going to shoot you back.

There are a few ways to exchange options, and you'll learn all of them. Let's get started now.

Hedge and Speculation

Hedging and speculation are the first two things you should learn before spending a single penny on trading options. These aspects are the ones that are going to get you going and how you're expected to handle trading options.

Hedging is when you fear something could go wrong. It doesn't mean that anything will go wrong; it's just a way to protect yourself (I mean your money) if things start to go wrong.

Hedging is the way to ensure your investment if rates start to fall. In other words, hiding is your defense against losing a lot of money. Large companies and institutional investors use hedging to cover themselves.

On the other hand, if you have no knowledge of the underlying asset (stock, bond, or commodity) when using options as a hedging strategy, then according to experts, you will certainly lose money. That's why you're trying to hedge too much to buy premiums on something you don't know. Thus instead of taking a gamble and growing your income, you're going to lose your insurance money.

However, if done properly, hedging is a perfect way to shield yourself from failure.

Next is speculation. But this is very dangerous.

There are three ways that any investor makes a profit: the price goes up, it goes down, and moves sideways (meaning, the price stays or goes up and down within the range).

A lot of money can be made from speculation. Speculation may be rendered by researching and analyzing the market, including assessing and forecasting patterns and finding out where the market is heading from the present point of view. This one can be a big advantage if you're familiar with the market and have good knowledge of the underlying asset.

But as I said before, speculation is very risky. An investor who wants to profit as a speculator must correctly predict the asset price trajectory (whether it will rise or fall), the timing of that direction, and the magnitude (the price will change by how much).

Advantages and Drawbacks in Trading Options

We accept that the options selling is difficult. But once you grasp it, it's going to be an ability that you know, like the back of your hand. The best part of options trading is that you can profit from the underlying asset's price range without directly investing in the asset.

As I mentioned earlier, investing in options is cheaper than investing in the actual asset. Plus, if you invest directly in the asset, you will have less leverage. In short, by selling options, you now have access to more money than you would have had initially.

If you add it up, leverage, capital, and so on, you can find that an investor will potentially make more money per actual dollar invested than investing directly in the asset. Often with options, an investor can only lose a fixed sum of money, which is effectively the premium he/she has paid.

Thus if you don't place anything in the premium, you're not going to lose everything. This thing is the safest to do if you're just trying to test the water, and you're not ready to go all in.

Another great benefit of Options Trading is that you can use hedging as an insurance strategy to shield yourself from losses that are getting too large. This aspect ensures that you can also shield yourself from extreme swings in the stock market. I would strongly recommend that you begin with as much hedging as possible to reduce your losses.

Another advantage is that you can make money even if the stock doesn't make money. It's because of the ability to trade up, down, or sideways to maximize your power and income. You'll see the stock price dropping several times, and you can still make a profit at the end of it.

Plus, commissions are much less active in trading options (now you know why stockbrokers advise you about it). And if you want to go through an online broker, those commissions are even smaller because they want to beat their competition.

Besides, the options trading is flexible. It helps you to respond based on where the price is going. It gives you the freedom to participate in more than one business as well. Thus you can invest in everything from agriculture to foreign currency. Plus, you don't have to spend a lot of money like large companies. All you need is a minimum sum, and you can start making money.

Last but not least, and this one is a biggie, the pace of having your profit in hand. Yeah, as soon as the stock increases, you'll get your benefit so that you can start investing in other markets or stocks. The pace of the market helps you to invest in more markets at the same time and make more money out of it. And unlike other forms of day trading, options trading is just a short-term bet. Thus even if you make an inaccurate prediction, you'll lose money within a few months instead of waiting for years to lose money because of that error.

Taxes are a detriment when it comes to trading options. Yeah, you're going to have to pay taxes on everything you do, except in those exceptional situations. So, make sure you fill out your IRA form to make sure you keep tax tabs before you start investing.

Moreover, unlike shares, there is no certificate of deposit when it comes to options. It's all paying rights, so it doesn't give you evidence of possession. Thus you will not justify to people the ownership of the stock unless it is a stock certificate.

And then there's a matter of ambiguity. It's a little frightening when you're investing in something you don't know. That's why most investors make sure they have an in-depth, detailed knowledge of what they're investing in because it can quickly turn into a gamble that isn't worth the winnings.

It's important to know your plan. And be sure to start small and slow to prevent losing high.

It's almost like driving a car. It's all scary when you're driving for the first time. But as you spend more and more time behind the wheel, you know the tricks of the trade, and you instantly become the best driver.

CHAPTER 3:

The Option Contract

Options Contract

An options contract sounds fancy, but it's a pretty simple concept.

- It's a contract. That means it's a legal agreement between a buyer and a seller.

- It allows the purchaser of the contract to purchase or dispose of an asset with a fixed amount.

- The purchase is optional–so the buyer of the contract does not have to buy or sell the asset.

- The contract has an expiration date, so the purchaser—if they choose to exercise their right—must make the trade on or before the expiration date.

- The purchaser of the contract pays a non-refundable fee for the contract.

A simple example illustrates the concept of an options contract.

Suppose you are itching to buy a BMW and you've decided the model you want must be silver. You drop by a local dealer, and it turns out they don't have a silver model in stock. The dealer claims he can get you one by the end of the month. You say you'll take the car if the dealer can get it by the last day of the month, and he'll sell it to you for $67,500. He agrees and requires you to put a $3,000 deposit on the car.

If the last day of the month arrives and the dealer hasn't produced the car, then you're freed from the contract and get your money back. In the event he does provide the vehicle at any date before the end of the month, you have the option to buy it or not. If you wanted the car, you could buy it, but of course, you can't be forced to buy the car, and maybe you've changed your mind in the interim.

The right is there, but not the obligation to purchase; in short, no pressure if you decided not to push through with the car's purchase. However, if you choose to let the opportunity pass since the dealer met his end of the bargain and produced the car, you lose the $3,000 deposit.

In this case, the dealer, who plays the contract writer's role, must follow through with the sale based upon the agreed-upon price.

Suppose that when the car arrives at the dealership, BMW announces it will no longer make silver cars. As a result, the prices of new silver BMWs that were the last ones to roll off the assembly line skyrocket. Other dealers are selling their silver BMWs for $100,000. However, since this dealer entered into an options contract with you, he must sell the car to you for the pre-agreed price of $67,500. You decide to get the car and drive away, smiling, knowing that you saved $32,500 and that you could sell it at a profit if you wanted to.

The situation here captures the essence of options contracts, even if you've never thought of haggling with a car dealer in those terms.

An option is, in a sense, a kind of bet. In the car example, the chance is that the dealer can produce the exact vehicle you want within the specified period and at the agreed-upon price. The dealer is betting also. He bets that the pre-agreed price is a good one for him. Of course, if BMW stops making silver cars, then he's made the wrong bet.

It can work the other way too. Let's say that instead of BMW deciding not to make silver cars anymore when your car goes onto the lot, another car crashes into it. Now your silver BMW has a small dent on the rear bumper with some scratches. As a result, the car has immediately declined in value. But if you want the car, since you've agreed to the options contract, you must pay $67,500, even though with the dent, it's only really worth $55,000. You can walk away and lose your $3,000 or pay what is now a premium price on a damaged car.

An Options Contract on the Stock Market

In the car case, the buyer is merely hoping to get the car they want at what they perceive to be a bargain price, although if BMW stopped making silver cars, they might sell it to a third party and then get a white one from the dealer. However, in most cases, the buyer wants the car. That isn't the case when it comes to options with stocks.

On the stock market, we are betting on the future price itself, and the shares of stock will be bought or sold at a profit if things work out. The critical point is the buyer of the options contract is not hoping to acquire the shares and hold them for an extended period like a traditional investor. Instead, you're hoping to make a bet on the stock price, secure that price, and then be able to trade the shares on that price no matter what happens in the actual markets.

Call options

A Call is a type of options contract that can purchase an asset at the agreed-upon amount at the designated time or deadline. The reason you would do this is if you felt that the price of a given stock would increase in price over the specified period. Let's illustrate with an example.

Suppose that Acme Communications makes cutting-edge smartphones. The rumors are that they will announce a new smartphone in the next three weeks to take the market by storm, with customers lined out the door to make preorders.

The current price that Acme Communications is trading at is $44.25 a share. The current pricing of an asset is another term for the spot price. Put another way; the spot price is the actual amount that you would be paying for the shares as you would buy them from the stock market right now.

Nobody knows if the stock price will go up after the announcement or if there's a release of the statement. But you've done your research and are reasonably confident these events will take place. You also have to estimate how much the shares will go up, and based on your research, you think it's going to shoot up to $65 a share by the end of the month.

You enter into an options contract for 100 shares at $1 per share. You pay this fee to the brokerage that is writing the options contract. In total, for 100 shares, you spend $100.

The price for an options contract is $100. This price is called the premium.

You don't get the premium back. It's a fee that you pay no matter what. If you make a profit, then it's all good. But if your bet is wrong, then you'll lose the premium. For the buyer of an options contract, the premium is their risk.

You'll want to set a price that you think will be lower than the level to which the price per share will rise. The amount that you agree to is called the strike price. For this contract, you set your strike price at $50.

Remember, exercising your right to buy the shares is optional. You'll only buy the shares if the price goes high enough that you'll make a profit on the trade. If the stocks never go above $50, say they reach $48, you are not obligated to buy them. And why would you? As part of the contract deal, buying them at $50 is required.

We'll say that the contract enters August 1, and the deadline is the third Friday in August. If the price goes higher than your strike price during that time, you can exercise your option.

Let's say that as the deadline approaches, things go as you planned. Acme Communications announces its new phone, and the stock starts climbing. The stock price on the actual market (the spot price) goes up to $60.

Now the seller is required to sell you the shares at $50 a share. You buy the shares, and then you can immediately dispose of these at a quality or optimal amount, or $60 a share. You make a profit of $10 a share, not taking into account any commissions or fees.

Put options

A Call option is the option to buy a stock if it reaches the strike price. Now let's look at the opposite situation. A Put is an option contract where you get the right but not the obligation to sell a stock before the deal expires. Suppose that Acme Communications looks to be heading to bad times, and the stock is trading at $44.25 a share. You bet that it's going to decrease to at least $35 a share, so you buy a Put option with a strike price of $35 a share. If you bet that the stock will decline in value and you're correct, let's say it drops to $30 a share, then you can make a $5 per share profit on the sale. If the stock meets the strike price, the Put's seller is obligated to purchase the stock at that price. In other words, even though the stock has dropped in value to $30 a share on the market, they must buy the shares from you at $35 a share.

Let's suppose that instead, it only drops to $38 a share. In this case, you don't have to sell and simply walk away from the deal having paid the premium. So, in this Call option situation, the premium is the only money that you risk on the buyer.

The seller of a Put option must buy the stock from you at the strike price if you exercise your option. If the strike price is $35, but for some reason, the stock crashes to $1, the Put's seller must buy the shares from you at $35.

The Concept of Moneyness

The term moneyness is used in Options trading to describe the financial status of an Option. An option is said to be in-the-money—or profitable to exercise if its strike price is lower than the underlying asset's price. For example, if you could exercise your rights to buy the underlying stock at the strike price to sell on the market for a profit immediately, it would be in-the-money.

However, the concept of moneyness has a few different aspects to it.

Remember that the strike price is the locked-in price that the underlying stock can be bought or sold for if exercised. Therefore, the strike price is an important factor in determining the options value as we can compare the options strike price with the actual market price of the stock. This relationship between the strike and actual market price determines the intrinsic value of the option and will be a determining factor:

- **At-the-money:** This is when the strike price and the stock price are the same, so it applies to both calls and puts.
- **Near the money:** As it is unlikely for the strike and actual price to match any close to equality, it is termed near the money.
- **In-the-money:** This is when the strike price in a Call option is below the actual stock price. On the other hand, with a Put option, the strike price is in-the-money above the stock price.
- **Out-of-the-money:** This is when a Call option strike price is above the stock price. With a Put option, the strike price will be out-of-the-money below the stock price.

Open Interest

An interesting metric often included in quote tables for Option contracts is an indicator depicting Open interest, the total number of outstanding options contracts. Open interest is tallied at the end of each day. Open interest is used as a metric for the measurement of market sentiment. It should not be misinterpreted as the number of options traded because it is not the same as volume, as many options are traded to close out existing positions.

However, if you are speculating in short-term trading of options, then Open Interest is an important metric as you will want as much market interest as you can get on your option. This indicator will make it easier to trade when you choose to exit the position as there will likely be many potential buyers.

Expiration and Exercise

Options expire at regular intervals determined by the expiration date, which is the date the option expires. Most options expire on the third Friday of a given month. However, some high-volume weekly options have expiration dates every Friday. The last time to trade the option is at the close of the market immediately before the option expires. Some European options close earlier (sometimes on a Thursday, but the closing time would be specified for the option, and most broker apps track the options expiry dates and send a notification, so you know):

The option period is the term used to denote the correct time until expiration, and it starts when the option is made (written) and ends on the expiry day. However, there are ways to stay in the position if you want to beyond the expiry date. If you want to maintain the position, you can roll by closing your current "soon to expire" open position and simultaneously make a new position at a different strike price or expiration.

Exercising your Rights

To exercise is the term used to cash in an option, but the vast majority of options are never exercised. But you should want to, and you have a Call option giving you the right to buy shares of ABC at $100 per share, and the stock is trading at $105, all you have to do is notify your broker that you want to exercise the options. When exercising your option to buy the stock, you will need to have your account's funds. Almost all brokers will require that you buy—pay for the stock—before you sell. Thus you will need sufficient funds in your account before you can exercise your position. Some brokers allow you to turn around and sell the stock immediately, and you may get away with selling the stock before you pay the broker, but that type of free-riding—is frowned upon.

Delivery and Settlement

When a Call option on a stock is exercised, the writer has to transfer the shares to the option buyer's account at the strike price. If the writer is not covered by already owning the stock, they must buy the shares in the open market.

Extrinsic and Intrinsic Value

Options have two primary sources of value. The intrinsic value is the option's strike price referring to the underlying asset price, and only if it is in-the-money. If it is not in-the-money, then there is no profit, so no value.

Time value, on the other hand, is known as extrinsic value. This value is the difference between the option's price and the amount of intrinsic value—the amount it is in-the-money. The logic behind this is that the amount that an option is in-the-money is its intrinsic value, the profit in case you claim it today.

But the option can be worth more today than the profit you would realize if you exercised it. This consideration is important when you are hedging as you do not want to exercise the option—take the profit. Instead, you value the time remaining on the insurance value of the option. This additional time value cannot be ignored as it explains why people will often hold onto options when they are profitable to exercise. Of course, they may just be riding a trend and hoping to end up with a larger profit. Nonetheless, it is important to realize that options do have both extrinsic value and intrinsic value. The more you understand the components of an option's price, the better you can value the option relative to your needs.

One additional concept of option value that we must know about is parity. When we refer to parity regarding an options value, we mean the point where an option is in-the-money but has no time value. Options generally don't reach parity until just before expiration.

Weighing Option Costs and Benefits

There are many advantages to trading using options, but you don't get all those benefits without taking on-board some risk element. A considerable risk that you have to accept is that options have a limited lifespan as they are limited by the expiry date. Now there are clear strategies that you must have in place when handling this risk, such as having an exit strategy. For example, your choices are, trade the option during the timespan of the option, expire the option on or before the expiry date or simply let the option expire. However, there can be a big problem with just leaving options to expire. For example, if the option is in-the-money at expiration, your broker may automatically exercise/assign the option. The problem here is that by exercising the valuable option, they have effectively converted a low-cost option position into a high-cost stock position, which you may not want or be able to afford.

Consequently, you need to monitor your options carefully and check for notifications from the broker platform regarding any in-the-money option positions, which are nearing the expiration date. You have to do this in anticipation of this likely change in your margin requirement. Alternatively, you want to make sure you have sufficient time to trade the option or make other adjustments such as rolling over trade to avoid buying the stock.

Risk of Leverage

Another significant risk to be aware of is that of leverage. Because options don't cost much as stock as they are simply a contract, thus they experience disproportionately larger percentage price gains in reaction to the far more expensive underlying stock's very small price movements. The huge benefit of this is that it results in large percentage wins when the underlying stock moves in the anticipated direction by even a small amount. The downside is that it also results in a 100% wipe-out of the investment if the stock moves by even the smallest amount in the wrong direction.

This situation is not necessarily an issue with beginners, or at least it shouldn't be, as the risk manifests itself mainly through trading too large a position size.

However, as beneficial as leverage is, you need to be aware that it can also be a double-edged sword, so be aware that leverage is a risk that needs to be addressed. One simple way to nullify or minimize this level of risk is to keep your position size small.

Trading Rules You Should Know

Whenever you begin trading a new market, you'll need to quickly become acquainted with the trading rules. Usually, your broker or their trading platform will prevent you from going wrong, but you shouldn't need to rely on them to keep you right.

We provide a shortlist of common basic rules for trading options that will hopefully help you through your initial trading executions and throughout your trading career:

- **Contract pricing:** In general options trading increments of $0.01, $0.05, and $0.10.
- **Option premium:** The price of the premium that you pay for an option is obtained by multiplying the option price offered by the multiplier. When trading in stocks, the multiplier value is usually based upon 100 shares of the underlying stock. Therefore,

when you purchase one option quoted at $2.80, you will have to pay $2,80 x 100 = $280 for the option, plus any broker commission.

- **Market conditions:** Different market conditions impact both the stock and options markets. These include the following:
  - ○ **Trading halts for security or the entire market:** If you find yourself holding an option for a halted stock, any options based on the stock will also be halted. This condition does not affect your rights or prevent you from exercising your contract rights. However, be aware that when this occurs before expiration, it may be difficult to trade the options but will not prevent you from exercising the option on or before the expiry date.
  - ○ **Fast trading conditions:** In fast-moving markets, stock prices can change rapidly, and you are likely to see quotes changing quickly. As a result, when you are placing an order, you might find significant delays. This condition can be because your bid is not falling out with the bid-ask spread, so it is ignored. Therefore, if necessary, you need to check and edit your order to make it more acceptable. Also, in fast-moving market conditions, make sure to use limit orders that are price-focused rather than market orders as you may end up paying more than you wanted.

Option Pricing Models

Option pricing theory uses all of the variables mentioned above to calculate the value of an option theoretically. It is a tool that allows trainers to get an estimate of an option's fair value as they incorporate different strategies to maximize profitability. Luckily, there are models that traders can use to implement option pricing strategies to their advantage. Three commonly used pricing models for option values are:

- The Black-Scholes Model
- Binomial Option Pricing Model
- Monte-Carlo Simulations

The Black Scholes Model

This pricing model won a Nobel Prize in economics because of its effectiveness. It was designed by the three economists, Fischer Black, Robert Merton, and Myron Scholes, in 1973. Originally used to price European options (meaning the option can only be exercised on the expiration date), this is a mathematical system that greatly influences modern option pricing. The pricing model helps differentiate gambling options by determining the option premium to be paid logically. It calculates the return on the income the investor is likely to earn less than the amount paid. The formulation of this amount uses the factors mentioned earlier in this chapter and others.

As this is primarily used to determine a European Call option, the formula used to calculate it looks like this:

SN(d1) – Xe - rt N(d2) = Call option Premium

The letter representations in this equation stand for:

S – Current asset price

N – A normal distribution

X – Strike price

r – risk-free interest rate

t – time of maturity

While this pricing system is great, it does have limitations. One of these limitations is that it assumes that factors like volatility and risk-free interest will remain constant, which is not the case. It also does not factor in other costs to set up the option.

Binomial Option Pricing Model

More commonly used to develop pricing for American options, this pricing system was developed in 1979. Even as popular as the Black Scholes Model is, this model is even more frequently used in practice because it is more intuitive. This pricing system assumes two possible outcomes—one where the outcome moves up and where the outcome moves down.

This system differs from the Black Scholes Model because it allows calculations for multiple periods, whereas the Black Scholes Model does not. This advantage gives a multi-period view, which is very advantageous to options traders.

This model makes use of binomial trees to figure out options pricing. These are diagrams with the main formula branching off into two different directions. This branching off is what gives the multi-period view for which this pricing system is famous.

For this pricing system to work, the following assumptions are made:

- There are two possible prices for the associated asset, hence the name of the pricing system. Bi means 2.
- The two possibilities involve the price of the asset moving up or down.
- No dividends are being paid on the asset.
- The rate of interest does not change through the life of the option.
- There are no risks attached to the transaction.

- There are no other costs associated with the option.

Just like with the Black Scholes Model, there is some limitation with those assumptions. Still, the pricing system is highly valuable in valuing American options because such options can be exercised at any time until the expiration date.

Monte Carlo Simulations

It is used in multiple fields across the board like science, engineering, and finance; this model allows the options trader to consider multiple outcomes due to random factors' involvement. It allows for the consideration of risk and unpredictability, unlike the first two pricing models. That's why it is also sometimes called multiple probability simulation.

CHAPTER 4:

The Psychology of an Options Trader

When it comes to making money trading options, you must remember that you must control your emotions at all times, which is easier said than done, especially if you are in the moment and have just taken an unexpected loss. Cultivating the proper mindset can be done with practice. Doing so will make it easier for you to face the early parts of your options trading career with the proper expectations regarding what sort of results you can expect from options trading. Specifically, this means that you will need to understand that investing in options isn't a quick and easy path to success and, rather, is sure to take plenty of dedication and hard work if you hope to reap the potential rewards.

The first step to finding success via options trading is to get your emotions in check. The best traders are robotic, they only rely on the facts, and they follow their trading plan 100 percent of the time. If you find yourself getting extremely emotional as far as trading is concerned, you must start by keeping a log of your emotions while trading and those emotions' results on your trading outcome. While this might seem unnecessary at first, you will be surprised how helpful having a clear outline of your patterns is when it comes to improving your overall trade percentage in the long term.

The fact of the matter is that if you ever hope to trade options successfully, you will need to know you can stick with your plan no matter what the emotional part of your mind is telling you to do. A good plan remains successful, not 100 percent of the time, or even 95 percent of the time, and instead manages to be successful roughly 60 percent of the time. While 60 percent is certainly enough to ensure you turn a profit, it is not enough that it allows for additional wiggle room in terms of letting your emotions talk you into going off the book at every turn. Remember, trading options is a numbers game, and keeping your emotions in check is key to not working with skewed data.

A lot of traders are largely focused on trading and earning profits. They are hardly ever concerned about the mindset and how they are supposed to handle emotions and feelings as they trade. Often, they focus on trades and celebrate when they win while feeling bad when they lose. This approach is not the best, according to experts.

It is crucial to be a successful trader to understand why some trades do not work out and why some lose money. By understanding why some traders lose money, it becomes possible to make adjustments to minimize as much as possible.

All traders, even the most experienced, win some trades and lose some. The difference is the number of losses and the reasons for the losses. Skilled traders can discern with relative accuracy the directions of the markets and chances of making winning trades. However, it is really difficult for anyone to perform better than the markets.

No trader can outperform the market, yet most traders are unable to grasp this simple principle. The most crucial initial step is to select winning trades. This skill needs to be learned. A trader should have an edge as this increases the chances of winning. If a trader has no edge, then he or she can only emerge victorious about half the time.

There are two things on which an options trader should focus. The first is to ensure to earn a profit of at least 50% or more. Also, money lost from any losing trades should not exceed that earned from winning trades. This condition calls for some skill development. An options trader should take time to develop the necessary skills on how to identify such trades.

You Can Weather the Storm

Options prices can move a lot throughout short periods. So, someone who likes to see their money protected and not losing any will not be suitable for options trading. Now, we all want to come out ahead, so I am not saying that you have to be happy about losing money to be an options trader. Options move big on a percentage basis, and they move fast. If you are trading multiple contracts at once, you might see yourself losing $500 and then earning $500 over a matter of a few hours. In this sense, although most options traders are not "day traders," technically speaking, you will be better off if you have a little bit of a day trading mindset.

Don't Make Emotional Decisions

Since options are, by their nature, volatile and very volatile for many stocks, coming to options trading and being emotional about it is not a good way to approach your trading. If you are emotional, you will exit your trades at the wrong time in 75% of cases. You don't want to make any sudden moves when it comes to trading options. As we have said, you should have a trading plan with rules on exiting your positions, stick to those rules, and you should be fine.

Be a Little Bit Math-Oriented

To understand options trading and be successful, you cannot be shy about numbers. Options trading is a numbers game. That doesn't mean you have to drive over to the nearest university and get a statistics degree. But if you do understand probability and statistics, you are a better options trader. Frankly, it's hard to see how you can be a good options trader without having a mind for numbers. Some math is at the core of options trading, and you cannot get around it.

You Are Market-Focused

You don't have to set up a day trading office with ten computer screens so you can be tracking everything by the moment, but if you are hoping to set up a trade and lazily come back to check it three days later, that isn't going to work either with options trading. You do need to be checking your trades a few times a day. You also need to be keeping up with the latest financial and economic news, and you need to keep up with any news directly related to the companies you invest in or any news that could impact those companies.

If the news does come out, you will need to decide if that news is favorable to your positions or not. Also, you need to be checking the charts periodically so you have an idea of where things are heading for now.

Options Traders Are Flexible

Most frequently, people do what they have been brainwashed to do, and they will trade Call options hoping to profit from rising share prices. If you are in that mindset now, you need to challenge yourself and begin trading in different ways to experience making money from declining stock prices, or in the case of Iron Condors, stock prices that don't even change at all. You need to be able to adapt to changing market conditions to profit as an options trader. So, don't entrap yourself by only using one method.

Take a Disciplined Approach

Don't just buy options for a certain stock because it feels good. You need to research your stocks. That will include doing fundamental analysis, paying attention to a stock's history, knowing what the typical ranges are for, and reading through the company's financial statements and prospectus. I suggest picking three companies to trade options on for a year and two index funds. The index funds require less research, but you should know those companies inside and out for the three companies you pick. Stick with them for a year, at the end of each year, evaluate each company. Then decide if you want to keep them and bring them forward into the following year's trades. If one company is not working out for you, then move on and try a different company.

Controlling Your Emotions (Trading Psychology)

Trading psychology is the mental state and emotions that determine the success or failure of trading options. It represents the aspect of your behavior that dictates the decisions you make when faced with a trade. Psychology is vital to any trade and can be compared to experience, knowledge, and skills in determining your success as a trader.

When you decide to start options trading, you need to grasp the concept of risk-taking and discipline that determines any trade implementation.

The two most common emotions are greed and fear.

Fear

At any given time, fear represents one of the worst kinds of emotions that you can have. Check-in your newspaper one day, and you read about a steep sell-off, and the next thing is trying to rack your brain about what to do next even if it isn't the right action at that time.

Many investors think that they know what will happen in the next few days, making them have a lot of confidence in the trade outcome. This consideration leads to investors getting into the trade at a level that is too high or too low, which in turn makes them react emotionally.

As the trader puts a lot of hope on the single trade, the level of fear tends to increase, and hesitation and caution kick in.

Fear is part of every trader, but skilled traders can manage fear. There are various types of fears that you will experience; let us look at a few of them. Have you ever entered a trade and all you could think about is losing? The fear of losing makes it hard for you to execute the perfect strategy or enter or exit a strategy at the right time.

To reduce the fear of trading, you need to accept losses. The probability of losing or making a profit is 50/50, and you need to accept this fact and accept a trade, whether it is a sell or a buy signal.

Greed

Greed refers to a selfish desire to get more money than you need from a trade. When the desire to get more than you can usually make takes over your decision-making process, you are looking at failure.

Greed is seen to be more detrimental than fear. Yes, fear can make you lose trades, but the good thing is that you get to preserve your capital. On the other hand, greed places you in a situation where you spend your capital faster than you return. It pushes you to act when you shouldn't be acting at all.

When you are greedy, you end up acting irrationally. Irrational trading behavior can be overtrading, overleveraging, holding onto trades for too long, or chasing different markets. The more greed you have, the more foolish you act. If you reach a point at which greed takes over from common sense, you are overdoing it.

CHAPTER 5:

Future Trading

Investing in bonds should be part of an overall strategy to achieve financial independence. To accomplish that, you need to know how to build a solid financial structure to deliver the desired result. Financial independence means having a guaranteed regular income to support your lifestyle without having to work.

Whatever the figure that comes works for you, financial independence means if you lose your primary source of income (wages, pensions, proceeds from a business), your life goes on normally without you having to seek a bailout. To build a solid or stable financial structure, you need to understand what it is and how to build one that works for you, and you need a proper foundation. That foundation is financial security. This security does not come from your job or your business. It comes from earning enough from other guaranteed (relatively risk-free) income sources to live your life normally if you lose your job or your business goes belly up. Thus your life is independent of an income you for which must work. You need to build the right financial structure to achieve financial stability through any economic cycle's ups and downs. This financial structure is built on having your money work for you. Your job is to convert a part of your earned income (that you work for) to passive income (that you don't work for)—building a structure whereby money works for you to eventually don't have to work for money anymore, but for love.

Whatever you are doing will come to an end someday. Your job will not last forever. You will leave it one way or the other, including mandatory retirement at a certain age. The marketplace is continuously evolving. Your line of business will be overtaken by new market trends, technology, etc., someday. The economy goes up and down, and this has an impact on your business. You need to build a financial support structure, a financial portfolio that will give you financial stability. This financial structure is made up of two plans:

Financial Security Plan

This plan is to secure your family financially in terms of sustaining your current standard of living. It is not to make you rich. Under this plan, investments are fixed-income investments whereby the returns are guaranteed, and the risk is almost zero. Investments in this plan include money market investments like fixed deposits, treasury bills, etc., that also include bonds.

Financial Growth Plan

This plan is to enable you to grow financially, become richer, essentially increase your net worth and raise your standard of living if you so desire. Returns under this plan are potentially higher than those under the financial security plan. The risks are also higher (higher risk, higher reward). You can make a lot of money and can also lose a lot of money. Investments under this plan include stocks, real estate, forex trading, etc., investments that appreciate. For those who desire to be very rich, there is a third plan:

Financial Abundance Plan

This plan is to make you very rich, a multi-millionaire, or even a billionaire (in dollars), whereby you can virtually afford anything you want. Investments under this plan, as you may have rightly guessed, are high risk and high reward. You can become very rich if it goes well, and you may be wiped out financially if it goes wrong, and you could accumulate huge debts while pursuing this dream. Such investments include investing in startups, think Apple, Facebook, Twitter, Google, LinkedIn, WhatsApp, YouTube, and Instagram. There is also another list— those that did not make it. This plan is often considered as part of the financial growth plan. So how do you tie all this together to build a solid financial structure? The answer is asset allocation.

Asset Allocation

You are working hard, saving before spending, and using your savings to invest. Where do you put the money? If you have a regular income, you need to start building the plans or portfolios, starting from the foundation, the financial security plan where the risk is virtually zero.

When you are just starting, you don't know much and are probably afraid of losing your hard-earned money. Every building starts from the foundation. Building a financial security plan is the starting point, and bonds are a valuable addition to your financial security plan. However, you need to understand that you need to build and keep both plans rather than build your financial security today and demolish tomorrow, which most people do. Like liquidating bond investments to build the financial growth plan, or worse still lend to a friend with a business idea.

Futures

Futures represent financial derivatives, and their value is determined by the changes in another asset's price. Thus its inherent value does not determine the futures price; rather, it depends on the asset's price being tracked by the futures contract. A key benefit of the futures market is that it is centralized and that people from all parts of the globe can create futures contracts electronically. The price of the merchandise will be determined by these futures contracts and the delivery time. Important information is included in each futures contract regarding the quantity and quality of the goods sold, the specified price, and how they will be transferred to the buyers.

The contract's overall worth is not paid by the individual who has bought or sold a futures contract. Rather, he pays a small percentage as a fee to take up an open position. For instance, if the Futures contract has a value of $350,000 and the S&P 500 is 1,400, then the initial margin payment that he makes is just $21,875. This margin is established by the exchange and may be modified at any point in time.

When the S&P increases to 1,500, the futures contract's value is going to be $375,000. Therefore, the individual will attain a profit of $25,000. However, if the index decreases to 1,390 from the initial level of 1,400, he will face a loss of $2,500 as the futures contract's value will now be $347,500. This loss of $2,500 has not yet been realized. The individual will not have to add more cash to his trading account.

When the index decreases to 1,300, the value of the Futures contract will be $325,000. The individual will experience a loss of $50,000. The broker will ask him to add more cash to his trading account because the initial margin of $21,875 is insufficient to cover the deficits. All futures contracts have a few similarities. However, different assets may be tracked by each contract. Hence, it is vital to assess the different markets.

Categories of Futures Markets

Agriculture:

- Grains
- Livestock
- Dairy
- Forest

Energy:

- Crude Oil

- Heating oil
- Natural gas
- Coal

Stock Index:

- S&P 500
- Nasdaq 100
- Nikkei 225
- E-mini S&P 500

Foreign Currency:

- Euro/USD
- GBP/USD
- Yen/USD
- Euro/Yen

Interest Rates:

- Treasuries
- Money markets
- Interest Rate Swaps
- Barclays Aggregate Index

Metals:

- Gold
- Silver
- Platinum
- Base Metals

Futures contracts can be traded on various assets and categories. However, a new trader needs to trade those assets of which that they are aware. For instance, if you have been involved in stock trading for some time, you should use stock indexes at the start of your futures contract trading. This knowledge would make it easier for you to comprehend the underlying asset. You need to comprehend the working of the futures market.

Once you have selected your category, you should determine which asset to trade. For instance, after choosing the energy category for trading futures contracts, you may focus on natural gas, coal, heating, or crude oil. Market trading takes place at different levels; hence, you should know different things, such as market requirements, liquidity, contract sizes, and volatility. Before trading in futures contracts, it is important to research the important aspects.

Investors making investments worth these tricks influence a large amount of money or those purchasing a significant number of products as price fluctuations can greatly impact the money spent on products. These "ticks" vary for different merchandise. The "ticks" of each commodity being traded in the futures and the minimum price fluctuation for each are distinct, depending on its kind.

CHAPTER 6:

Forex Trading

The FOREX market can be imagined from two different points of view. The first image is certainly positive; that is the vision of a financial market that can offer anyone the possibility of easily making profits: an opportunity to round up one's salary or even transform investment into real work. The second image is negative. The FOREX can indeed be seen as a money-eating system, illusory and bankrupt.

In reality, both visions are wrong. FOREX is a system that allows for gains in the medium-long term, but only for those who decide to implement a strategy correctly, dedicating both money and time to the market. Trading is complicated and difficult, but not a random activity. This concept is very important as it means that any fluctuation could be anticipated correctly by investors. However, several theories and tools can simplify their tasks. But even these tools require time and money to function properly and send the trader's right signals.

The brokers, with the advent of the internet, have made different platforms available to their users. They have some fundamental indicators and oscillators and translate the market's oscillatory movements on the charts to simplify their reading.

However, it is necessary always to consider the risks associated with the trading activity. Investments in the financial market offer as many profits as losses. It is impossible to eliminate the harmful components, which may be due to incorrect strategies, lateral phases of the market, and normal competition present in FOREX. Therefore, the losses must be received according to a positive vision, accepting them as much as the profits. There are indeed few traders who succeed in making profits in the long run. Still, it is also true that few investors rationally enter the market without being carried away by revenge or by the will to carry out simple attempts to become rich.

Once the strategy has been implemented, it is necessary to follow it assiduously unless it presents some gaps and requires instrumental corrections.

The concept is to "play" responsibly, that is, to invest one's capital with the knowledge that success and failure rates can be almost similar. The first objective must be to develop a strategy capable of minimizing the risks of the trader.

Currency Pairs and Pips

As we know, the basic of the FOREX market is buying and selling currencies. Trading is always by pair of currencies. We have "base currency", and the other side is the "counter currency". We need to know the information about how much the exchange rate color.

For example, EUR/USD has a quote of 1.24. That means 1 EUR is worth $1.24. EUR is base currency. USD is the counter currency. That is how the FOREX market works. The currency pair is necessary to form for the traders to do a transaction. These are some major currency pairs on which traders always focus.

Majors

EUR/USD. The Euro and U.S. Dollar currency pair is the most popular and widely traded of the majors. The Euro was introduced in 1999, and it's a relatively strong currency that represents all the major countries in Europe that are part of the European Union. Although Brexit is dominating recent headlines, even with Britain as a part of the European Union, it has maintained its currency, the Great British Pound. Hence, the Euro is the currency used by members of the E.U. on the continent.

When it comes to this currency pair, you will want to watch moves by the European Central Bank or ECB and the U.S. Federal Reserve. Of course, in any of the majors, you will be looking at moves by the U.S. Federal Reserve.

The biggest strength of this currency pair from the perspective of a small retail trader is that it is a highly liquid financial asset that often has substantial volatility. In recent years, the volatility and the magnitude of moves (on average) have decreased somewhat, but it's still a rather strong average pip movement of 200 pips. Since this currency pair is so liquid, getting in and out of trades fast will not be an issue. This currency pair is certainly a good choice for beginners or a trader of any level.

USD/JPY. This binomial is the U.S. Dollar and Japanese Yen currency pair. Japan isn't quite the monolith in the 1980s when everyone thought Japan would economically take over the entire world. However, Japan still maintains a large and powerful economy dominated by well-known companies like Toyota, Subaru, and Sony. One factor that is important when considering this currency pair is that Japan remains one of the world's largest exporting nations. Thus it's a frequently traded and highly liquid currency because all that exporting means that people have to convert dollars into Yens and vice versa all the time. The interest rate is low, making this currency pair more attractive for holding over longer periods.

GBP/USD. As we mentioned above, despite being a long-time member of the European Union, Great Britain held onto its currency rather than adopt the Euro in 1999. Now that Britain may exit the European Union, for good or for worse, this probably means that the Great British

Pound is here to stay for the foreseeable future. We noted earlier in the book that this was once (and sometimes still is) referred to as the cable, as currency trading between the United States and Great Britain went on via electronic cable under the Atlantic Ocean starting in the late 19th century. Brexit may introduce a lot of volatility in this currency pair and any currency pair involving GBP, so traders may want to pay attention to it, at least for the near future. Even after Brexit is finalized, there is likely to be some extra volatility introduced into GBP currency pairs' price movements if it ever actually is. Whether in favor of the GBP or against it, that is not a question relevant to the FOREX trader. You are not favoring one currency over another because you like it. You are picking currencies based on what works in a given trade.

USD/CHF. CHF is the ticker symbol (to use a stock analogy) for the Swiss Franc. Switzerland is another country maintaining its currency, and given Switzerland's strong banking presence, it's an important currency despite the relatively small size of the country and its economy. Traders consider the Swiss Franc to be an important currency during times of economic trouble or international crisis. When there are global problems, in most cases, the Swiss Franc can be expected to increase against the U.S. Dollar because the demand for the Franc rises as people look for a relatively safe place to put their money in. If there is an economic crisis that you happen to experience, remember this and bet on the Swiss Franc against the dollar. In times of uncertainty, economic downturn, or crisis, the Swiss Franc may also do well against several other currencies such as the Japanese Yen. The USD/CHF pair sometimes goes by the nickname "Swissie."

USD/CAD. Although Canada has a relatively small population compared to the European Union, Japan, and the United States, its economy enjoys outsized importance because it shares a border with the United States. A large amount of trade goes on between the two countries. Canada has many natural resources that it exports, such as oil, natural gas, and timber, which again maintains an outsized level of importance in economics and currency trading. Due to its direct relationship with the United States, the USD/CAD currency pair can be a good trade, even though it doesn't play as large a role in the markets as the EUR/USD currency pair. When relations between Canada and the United States are good, volatility can decrease for this currency pair. When there are some difficulties, this can lead to increased volatility making it more attractive to trade. Canada has large exports of coal, raw aluminum, iron ore, gold, and copper ore. So, to get a feel for how the movement of the Canadian dollar may be trending concerning other currencies, you might want to see if the prices of these commodities are rising or falling. Since Canada is exporting these materials, this generally means that rising commodity prices are good for Canadian currency.

AUD/USD. Australia is a diverse and highly modern economy, but like Canada, its economic fortunes are often influenced very heavily by the export of natural resources. When it comes to Australia, you will want to pay attention to iron ore and rare earth metals, along with coal.

When commodity prices are rising, Australia's fortunes are often rising with it, but when they are declining, Australia's fortunes are probably going down as well. When you are trading any currency pair involving the Australian dollar, you'll want to look at various commodities' prices. Still, especially coal and iron ore, to see how they are going. Australia also exports large amounts of gold, petroleum, and wheat. So good pricing moves for these commodities may put the Australian dollar in a position to rise against other currencies.

NZD/USD. The last of the majors is the currency pair between the New Zealand Dollar and the U.S. Dollar. The New Zealand economy isn't as large as the others we've considered, and it's highly dependent on tourism and the export of agricultural products. It is a leading exporter of dairy products as well as lamb and other meats. If dairy prices rise on commodities markets, this can bode well for any currency pair involving the NZD.

Crosses

If the USD is not in the currency pair, these are called crosses. There are crosses for each of the currencies from major economies, such as the Euro or the Japanese Yen. The majors enjoy the highest trading volume and are, therefore, the most liquid currency pairs that you can trade, but there are several crosses with high trading volume, which can be good to trade.

First, let's look at some of the Euro crosses:

- **EUR/JPY:** As you might imagine, there is a lot of trade that goes on between these two major economies. As a result, this can be a good currency pair to trade. When exports are in favor, Japan might have an edge, particularly when electronic components are considered.

- **EUR/CHF:** This is the Euro and Swiss Franc cross pair. The thing to look for here is the overall economic situation and whether there are any international tensions.

Generally speaking, if people are looking for a safe refuge for their money, the Swiss Franc will be it. So, when times are tough, you might look for increased volatility with this currency pair, and you might also look for the Swiss Franc to be rising in value against the Euro.

CHAPTER 7:

Swing Trading

Swing trading is the art and science of profiteering from the price movements of a security over the short-term, from a couple of days to a maximum of one month. Swing traders can be individuals or institutions like hedge funds. These traders look at low-risk opportunities available to themselves before taking any bets in the markets. They try to find out undervalued companies, go long on them and try getting the lions' share of the trade once there is an upswing. They are also known to short companies that they believe are overbought for the time being and ride the wave to the downside.

Picking out a good type of investment can be hard. You want to pick out one that will bring you a good amount of profit in the process, but you also need to limit your risk, or you could lose out on everything in the long run. You have a variety of options when it comes to trading. You can choose to invest in the stock market over the long-term or with day trading. You can start your own business and let this be your investment. And you can also work in real estate or other similar investments.

If you want to have the potential to earn a lot of money by investing in a short amount of time, then you may want to consider working with swing trading. Swing trading tries to capture the gains as possible with any stock, or financial instrument, within an overnight hold over several weeks. This investment is a short-term one, which means you will not hold onto your position for many years, but it gives you a little more time than you would have with day trading and some other investment options. The traders who work in swing trading may use either the intrinsic or the stock's fundamental value while also looking at the patterns and price trends that come with the stock to help them make good decisions.

So, how does swing trading work compared to some of the other investment opportunities? To start, all traders need to act quickly to find situations where a particular stock has a big potential to move upwards in a short amount of time. For instance, some unusual upward trend is about to happen, something that others may miss out on, but a trader will recognize when looking at the trends, the news, and other information.

If you can trade on these trends, purchasing the stock when it is at a lower price, holding onto it for up to a few weeks, and then selling when that huge upward trend ends up happening.

For the most part, swing trading occurs with day traders, especially individuals and those who work at home in this market. Most large institutions will be too big and have too many assets to move out of the stocks quickly enough to make this worth their time. This is one of the benefits of being an individual trader; you can move around the market much faster than big companies can, allowing you to earn a lot of profit in the process.

A swing trader will either hold a short or a long position, and they need to hold this position for one night up to a few weeks. The goal here is to get a larger profit than you could with day trading by hoping the market moves up even more. With swing trading, you will assume that larger price moves and ranges will occur, which means that you need to pick your position carefully to minimize your risks. And when you work with time frame charts, you would rely on a bit larger, such as hour, daily, and weekly charts based on what you think the market will do.

How Swing Trading Works

The first thing that you need to do is pick out a good broker to work with. These brokers can make a big difference in how well your trades will go overall. They can place the trades for you, offer you some advice when needed, and a lot more. There are various types of brokers you can work with, and it often depends on the features you would like, how much you want to spend, and how much help you will need in the process. Do some research on the best brokers in your area to help you see the best results.

You also need to figure out which analysis tools you would like to use. You need to have a few in place because this helps you to understand which trend is coming up better than just relying on one at a time. We will take a look at some of the tools you can use for swing trading and the strategies to pick the one that is the best for you.

Once you pick out the analysis tool you want to use, you need to spend some time researching it and learning exactly how it works. Your broker will be able to provide you with a few of these tools, so that can make things easier, but you should also look at some of your own. The more research you can do before entering the trade, the better chance you will have to catch the trend and make the biggest profit.

Next, you need to take some time and pick out which strategy you would like to use. Several strategies work well, but you need to go with one strategy and stick with it the whole time. Each strategy is different and will require you to enter the market differently, so you need to stick with one strategy and learn how to use it correctly.

Choosing a good strategy is probably going to be one of the hardest things to do. They all work differently and each require you to look at the charts differently from the others. And if you mess up with a strategy or you try to mix them up in the middle of a trade, you will end up losing a lot of money in the process. This situation can be stressful for someone new to the swing trading business. Ensure you fully learn how each strategy is supposed to work and even discuss some of them with your broker ahead of time to help you pick the right one.

You also have to take the time to get started with your trades. Your broker will be able to help you out with this part. They can either give you advice on the trades that you will work with, or you can tell them the rules you want to follow. Either way, they should put the trades in for you since they can quickly get the work done.

When placing your trades, make sure that you place your stop points. You need a stopping point for losing and earning money. These are points where you will exit the market and reduce your risk. If the market ends up going down to your stop loss point, it means it is time to get out of the market. Some beginners may want to sit around and wait to see if their losses will reverse, but this allows the emotions to get into the mix and can result in a big loss of money. Once your market reaches your preset stop-loss point, it is time to exit the market and cut your losses.

You need a stopping point on the other side of things as well. This condition helps you get your profits and know when you should leave the market, even if it goes back up. Since you are trading over a short amount of time, you want to ensure that you will reach your profits without losing money if things reverse. Putting this stop point in place will help you make as much profit as possible while also reducing your risk.

When the trade has been successful, you can be done with your first round of swing trading. Some of the trades will happen overnight, and others will take a few weeks to accomplish, but most of the time, you will complete your trade and earn your profit in a relatively short period. You can then take your profit and move on to your next trade.

Getting started with swing trading is a great option. It can help you make a lot of money quickly, but there is a level of risk that you will need to learn to deal with. Understanding how to get into the market, read the charts, and so on will help you get the results you would like. When you are ready to get started with swing trading, make sure to follow some of these great tips:

Pick an Easy Strategy

Some beginners think that complex strategies are best to increase their profits. But these complex strategies can be confusing and overwhelming for someone who is just beginning. Go with a simple strategy, at least until you learn more about the market.

Start in One Place

Many beginner traders will start by trying out too many markets at once. This situation can make it hard to know what you are doing. Stick with one market and one pattern and concentrate on that for now.

Don't Forget a Stop Loss

That is one of the main reasons that a trader will lose all their money. They will forget the stop loss and not watch the market enough, resulting in a huge loss in the process. Always use stop orders to help you reduce your risk.

Trade Both Directions

The best way to make money in swing trading is to trade on both sides of the market. If you spend your whole-time trading on the long side, you will miss half of your trading opportunities.

Keep a Good Risk-to-Reward Ratio

This ratio needs to be at least one to three. Remember that you are trading short-term, so you will not make a ton of money in the process. You can make a decent profit, but you won't make many thousands over this time. Ensure that you stay with a good risk-to-reward ratio to make some money without losing everything.

Don't Trade Inside a Vacuum

One issue that a beginner will face is that they will only take a look at a chart or two, and then they forget what is going on elsewhere. You need to look through the news to see what information will change the value of a stock. You need to look at various charts. You need to get your information from as many places as possible to help you get the best results.

Look at Market Indicators

These market indicators can help you determine how your trading will go and not what you should avoid looking through.

CHAPTER 8:

Stock Options Trading

ETF Options vs. Index Options

In 1982, future stock index trading started. It was the first time that traders could exchange a specific index themselves, rather than the firms' securities that contained the market index. First came stock index futures options, then index options that could be traded in stock accounts.

The following were index funds that allowed investors to purchase and retain a specific stock index. The recent growth boom started with introducing the ETF and was followed by trading options on a large portion of these new ETFs.

ETFs and ETF Options

An ETF is simply a mutual fund traded like an individual portfolio. As a result, an investor may purchase or sell an ETF that tracks or represents a particular segment of markets at any time during the trading day. The widespread proliferation of ETFs has also significantly increased investors' ability to take advantage of a wide range of unique opportunities. Investors can now take long and short positions—as in many cases, the following types of securities are leveraged in long or short situations:

- Domestic and Foreign Stock Indexes (small-cap, growth, large-cap, value, sector, etc.)
- Currencies (euro, yen, pound, etc.)
- Bonds (treasury, corporate)
- Commodities (commodity indexes, financial assets, physical commodities, etc.)

As with index options, some ETFs have attracted many trading options, whereas most have attracted very little.

One reason for considering volume is that numerous ETFs go the same indexes or similar to direct index options. You will also find which vehicle provides the best choice for liquidity and bid spreads.

Index Options

The list of options on different market indices allowed several traders to trade with one transaction for the first time in the broader financial market segment. The Chicago Board Options Exchange offers listing options on more than 50 domestic, foreign, industry, and volatility indexes.

The first thing to note about index options is that the underlying index itself does not trade. It is a measured value and is only available on paper. The options allow only one to speculate about the price direction of the underlying index or cover all or part of a portfolio that might closely correlate with that particular index.

Key Differences

There are several significant differences between index options and ETF options. The most important of these is that trading options on ETFs may lead to the necessity of taking or providing shares of the underlying ETF (which some may or might not find to be a benefit). This consideration does not apply to index options.

This difference is due to index options being "European" and cash, while ETF options are "American" options and are settled into shares of the underlying assets.

American options are also subject to "early practice," which means they can be exercised at any time before expiry, triggering the underlying safety trade. This opportunity for early practice and a put in the ETF can have substantial implications for a trader.

Index options may be purchased and sold before expiry; however, they cannot be exercised because the actual index does not include trading. As a result, there are no early exercise issues when trading an index option.

Special Considerations

The volume of trading options is a critical factor in determining which way to conduct a trade. This evaluation applies in particular to indexes and ETFs that follow the same or similar protection.

For example, if a trader wished to reckon with options on the S&P 500 index's direction, he or she can choose from several options. Each monitor of the S&P 500 Index is SPX, SPY, and IVV. Both SPY and SPX trade in large volumes and enjoy also the sealed bids. This combination of high importance and tight spreads indicates that investors can freely and actively sell these two securities.

CHAPTER 9:

Swing Trading with Options

The most straightforward way to trade options is to make a bet on the stock market's direction and buy Call or Put options accordingly. Most beginning options traders will have to start with this method because more advanced strategies are closed off to beginning options traders. However, that isn't all bad because you should feel for the options market before attempting more complicated trades.

What Swing Trading Is

The type of trading that we are going to talk about can loosely be described as swing trading. If you are not familiar with it, swing trading is a simple trading philosophy, where the idea is to trade "swings" in the market prices. There is nothing special about swing trading in a commonsense kind of way because it's a buy-low and sell-high trading method with stocks. You can also profit from a stock when the price is declining by "shorting" the stock.

So, what distinguishes swing trading from other types of trading and investing? The main important distinction is that swing trading is different from day trading. A day trader will enter their stock position and exit the position on the same trading day. Day traders never hold a position overnight.

Swing traders hold a position at least for a day, which means they will hold their position at a minimum overnight. Then they will wait for an anticipated "swing" in the stock price to exit the position. This time frame can be days to weeks or out to a few months at the most.

A swing trader also differs from an investor since, at the most, the swing trader will be getting out of a position in a few months. Investors are in it for the long haul and often put their money in companies they strongly believe in. Alternatively, they are looking to build a "nest egg" over a time of one to three decades or even more.

Swing traders don't particularly care about the companies they buy stock in. They are simply looking to make a short-term profit. So, although swing traders may not be hoping to make an instant profit like day traders, they are not going to be hoping for profits from the long-term prospects of a company. A swing trader is only interested in changing stock prices. Even the reasons behind the changes in the stock prices may not be important. So, whether it's

Apple or some unknown company, if it is in a big swing in stock prices, the swing trader will be interested.

The chart below shows the concept of swing trading. If you are betting on falling prices, you can earn profit following the chart's red line. If you are betting on increasing prices, you will follow the upward trending blue line. A bet on falling prices is often referred to as short, while a bet on rising prices means you are long on the stock. Of course, this is another difference between swing trading and investing; investors don't short stocks.

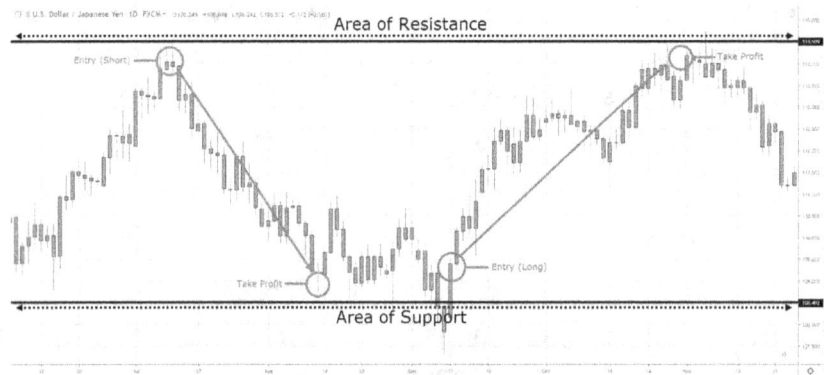

Swing trading can be used in any financial market. In the chart above, we are showing a chart from the Forex (currency exchange) market. The principles are the same, so the specific market we are talking about doesn't matter, which is why it works with options.

Support and Resistance

An important concept often used by swing traders is spotting support and resistance. Support refers to a local low price of the stock. It's a pricing floor that, for the time being, the stock price is not dropping below. To find support, you just draw straight lines on the stock chart. The share price should touch the support level at least twice to be a good level of support.

Resistance is a local high price. So, this is a high price level that the stock is not able to break above. Again, expect it to touch the resistance level at least twice and drop back down before you consider a given share price for the resistance level.

As the share price moves between support and resistance, there are opportunities to buy-low at the support level and then sell-high at the resistance level. And you can do the reverse in the case of shorting a stock. You can enter your position at the relatively high resistance level, then exit your position at the support level.

Of course, support and resistance will not be reasonable price levels for all time, and stocks will often "break out" of support or resistance. This situation happens when the share price starts declining and goes below the support level or breaking out above the uptrend's resistance level. There can be more opportunities to make a profit. But, when a stock price is stuck between support and resistance levels, we say it "ranges".

Trade with the Trend

The best thing to happen to a swing trader (or a trader of straight Call and Put options) is for a stock to enter into a unidirectional trend. So, it could be a trend in upward prices, giving you a chance to make large profits before it starts reversing. Alternatively, of course, trends can head downwards, opening up opportunities for those who are shorting the stock.

Trends can exist in many different time frames. It might only last part of a day, or it could last weeks and even months. Learning to spot trends and take advantage of them, knowing when they will come to an end, comes with experience and education. A new options trader can benefit by studying educational materials related to both swing and day trading. Hence, they know what to look for in stock charts to spot trends worth getting into and spot a trend reversal, which would eat up your profits.

The chart below of AutoZone stock is a simple example of this concept. It's a dream trade, with prices going steadily up with time. But remember, nothing lasts forever.

Trading with a trend is something you'll want to look for as an options trader. The time scale of the trend will be something important, of course, because you will be concerned about time decay when trading options. Time decay is a concept that a swing trader does not have to worry about.

So rather than being beholden to specific rules, like saying you will trade options like a day trader or like a swing trader, an options trader must be flexible. You will need to be ready to take advantage of very short-term moves in stock price that only last for a day or less, and you'll also want to be in trades that can last days to weeks or even months.

Swing Trading Options

Since options are time-limited, they are a natural fit for the concept of swing trading. Although many of the advanced strategies attempt to take out the direction of share price movement from the equation, if you are buying single Call or Put options to make a profit, you're behaving at least in a qualitative sense as a swing trader.

Since Put options gain in value when stock prices are declining, buying Put options is like shorting the stock. It's quite a bit more accessible, however. To short stock, you must have a margin account to borrow shares from the broker. Shorting a stock's basic idea is to borrow shares from the broker when the stock price is relatively high and sell them. After this, the trader will wait for the share price to drop. When the share price is low enough to profit, the trader will buy the shares back and return them to the broker.

Of course, shorting stock using options is far easier. The reason is you never have to buy the stock to make a profit from the declining price. You simply profit from the prices of Put options, which will increase as the stock price goes down.

Going Long on a Stock

If you believe that the price of a stock will rise, you want to buy Call options. So, the Call options represent the most straightforward or commonsense way to trade options. When you buy a Call option, you are betting on that stock. Another way to say this is that you are bullish on the stock.

A good way to go about trading options is to pick a few companies and limit yourself to trading them. The reason is that you will need to be paying attention to the markets, company news, and general financial news for any option that you invest in. If you spread yourself too thin, you will not stay on top of things and find yourself getting caught up in losing trades. The best approach is to keep your trading limited in scope to know what is going on. That doesn't mean you only trade a single Call option; you might trade many of them on the same stock.

There are two ways to go about swing trading options. The first way is to look for ranging stocks that are trapped in between support and resistance. Then you can trade Call and Put options that move with the swings. So, the idea of this type of trading is very simple. First, you need to study a stock of interest and determine the price levels of support and resistance. Then, when the price drops to the support level, you buy Call options. Now hold them until the price goes back up near resistance. It can be a good idea to exit your trades before the price gets to resistance so that you don't end up losing some of your potential profits if the price reverses before you get rid of the options.

Trend trading Call options can also be very lucrative. In this case, you are looking for important news and developments related to the stock or even the economy at large. For example, when a company announces that it had big profits, this can be an opportunity to earn money with Call options, as the price will go up by large amounts as people start snapping up the stock. When trading in this fashion, you're going to need to know how to spot trend reversals. The idea is the same when you identify a trend in the making; you buy Call options and then ride the trend until you are satisfied with the profit level and sell the options.

CHAPTER 10

Financial Leverage Concept in Options Trading

Financial Leverage

The process of using borrowed capital (or debt) to increase the shareholder's return on their investments or equity in capital structure is called "financial leverage" or "trading on equity". The financial leverage analyzed by the firm is intended to earn more return on the fixed charge funds rather than their costs. The surplus will increase the owner's equity, whereas the deficit will decrease the return on the owner's equity. Financial leverage affects the EPS (Earnings per share). When the EBIT increases, then EPS increases.

For example, if the firm borrows a debt from creditors for $1,000 at 7% interest per annum, i.e., $70, and invests this debt to earn a 12% return on this, i.e., $120 per annum. The difference of surplus, i.e., $50, which is after interest payment is made to the firm's creditors, will belong to its shareholders or owners. It is referred to as profit from financial leverage. Conversely, if the firm earns a 5% return, the firm has a loss of $20 (i.e., $70 - $50) to the shareholders.

Highly leveraged companies may be at risk of bankruptcy if they cannot pay their debt. Still, it can increase shareholder's return on their investment, and there are tax advantages associated with leverage.

Financial Leverage Ratio = EBIT / EBT

The financial leverage ratio is used to analyze the Capital structure and financial risk of the company. It explains how the fixed interest-bearing loan capital affects the operating profit of the firm. If EBIT is more than EBT, this ratio becomes more than 1.

Types of Leverages

Operating Leverage

Operating leverage is just concerned with the investment activities of an individual firm. It is about the incurrence of the fixed cost of operation in a company's income stream. The operating price can either be fixed, semi-fixed, variable as well as semi-variable. The fixed fee is contractual, and it is subject to time. It does not necessarily have to change when the sales change, and it is supposed to be paid despite the number of sales.

Financial Leverage

It is a relation to the combination of debts and equity in the capital format of a company. When there are financial charges in existence, the financial leverage will as well exist. The business costs should not depend on the operating profits in any way. The sources from which the funds that help to boost an investment come can be put in categories. The funds can either be having a fixed charge, and some may not be having the fixed financial cost. Debentures, preference shares, bonds as well as long-term loans have a fixed financial burden. Equity shares are known to have no fixed charge at all.

Combined Leverage

If you bring both the operating leverage and the financial leverage together, they will develop the combined force. It concerns the risk of not covering up the total amount of the fixed charges when a firm can fully cover the operating and financial burdens; that is when the term combined leverage comes in. The higher the fixed operating cost and the financial charges, the higher the combined force level.

Working Capital Leverage

In case of a decrease in a particular asset's investment, there will be an increase in profit. When there are many investors in the market and dealing with the same trade, there will be decreased profit. When there is a decrease in an asset's investment, its risk will go high. That means that risks, as well as returns, have direct relations. When the probability of risk goes up, there is a likely hood that the profit will increase.

An individual firm's ability to increase the current stock's change on the firm's returns is working capital leverage. It is so when there is an assumption that the liabilities are constant.

The Risks of Incorrect Use

Limited Growth

When you have a loan, the lending company will expect that you will pay in the period that was agreed upon when you were getting the loan. They hope that you will be on time and no failures should come along the way. It is a problem when an investor borrows money for a long-term project that will not generate some income immediately. That will make them find an alternative to paying the loan to avoid breaching the contract. If the payment period has come, and the investor has no returns, paying the mortgage can be a burden in one way or the other. When you decide to start paying the loan, you will use the money you borrowed to pay it back. When that happens, you will have less money for financing your operations. You will not be in a position to implement full-on the plan that you had. That means that you can have retardation, and you will not execute your plan fully. When investing, you need a plan and set deadlines for the completion to remain on your focus. When you have to pay the loan with the money you borrowed, you will not hit your deadlines. That will mean that you will experience limited growth, and you may not have the potential to continue as per the plan.

Losing Assets

When you cannot pay loans and are highly leveraged, that can lead to your assets' conspirator. There is no way that a company should pay capital sourcing from equity. When that happens, and the lender expects you to pay your loan in time, they can decide to take some of your assets to stand in for the loan. The assets can be of a similar value or a value higher than your investment. When in a loan, the company is supposed to pay the lender before any other deductions. Repossession of assets can happen if there is no money to pay the lender in time.

If the lender has to be paid even before its employees, the employees may look for another option and quit working with you. That will make you lose assets of value, and you will be left stranded.

Inability to Get More Financing

Before a lender gives you money to invest in any trade, they will first check whether you have any other loan. They will do that to establish how secure their payment is with you. If you are in debt, no lender will want to lend you more because they are not sure whether you will be in a position to clear their debt. They will access the risk associated if the company goes down, meaning there will be no one to pay their loan. When a company goes down, it is declared bankrupt, which means that the lender cannot legally claim their money. No lender will agree to put them last on your loan list since they know they will be the last to be paid.

An Investor Will Not Be in a Position to Attract Equity

When a company has high leverage, they are not able to increase the equity capital amount. And it is rare for an investor to give money to a business that has bid records of unclear loans. In the same way, lenders will avoid providing more money to a company with high amounts of investments, and in the same way, investors avoid such business. You will lose the potential of attracting investors when you have a lot of pending debts. When a lender knows they are the last in your line to be paid their loan, they will not find it comfortable to lend you. If you get an investor to give you at any chance, they will demand a significant percentage in terms of ownership in return for lending you the money.

Advantages of Leverage

Increase in Profit

Leverage will earn you more benefits without necessarily having to put in more effort. Since it is borrowed money, you do not have to toil so much to earn it; instead, you look for a lender. When you fulfill the requirements, the lender will finance you, and you will have to repay when the period lapses. When you inject more capital into a business, it will likely give you more returns under favorable market conditions.

An Increase in Capital Efficiency

When you increase the amount of money in a particular transaction can lead to a rise in productivity on how you use your capital. You need to consider capital as an asset, and it can increase the level of yields. When you take a loan, you will increase the amount of money, and you will raise the level of efficiency.

A Tool that Mitigates Against Low Volatility

Leverage is a great approach that can be put in place to mitigate the effect brought about by low volatility. Volatile trade is known to deliver huge profits in the Forex market. It can deliver good benefits from a small transaction and shield against the effect of low volatility. A small entity can become a big firm with the help of leverage. Leverage will help you to capitalize on the small significant levels of movement in the trading price.

Disadvantages of Leverage

Lower Liquidity

It is worth noting that a lot of individual stock options dint has many volumes. There are cases where one is forced to own very few stocks. The aspect present in all the options will trade at different strikes of payments and expectations. The particular option will be forced to have less volume unless it is one of the most popular stock indexes or stocks.

High Spreads

The art of lacking liquidity among these trading options causes higher spreads. The aspect is detrimental because one is forced to pay more indirect costs while using this trade option. The element is linked to the fact that they will be spreading the trade when using the opportunity.

Higher Commissions

When one is operating with such organizations, one is forced to pay using commission terms. In other words, one has to pay a certain amount of commission for each dollar that is invested.

The demerit is worsened because the option has very many options that forced one to have many spreads.

CHAPTER 11:

Advanced Concepts and the Options Greeks

The main factors that impact an option's price go into a mathematical model that governs options pricing. These are labeled as parameters with Greek letters. Although most of us have an aversion to anything "Greek," an options trader should be familiar with the Greeks, which are parameters you can look up at any time when trading options. As we will see, it is not necessary to get into the mathematical details of how they work behind the scenes. You can simply read off the numbers and then interpret them according to simple rules. Let's go through each of them in turn.

Delta and the Price of the Underlying Stock

The first "Greek" to consider is Delta, a parameter that tells you how an option's price will move with a price change in the underlying stock. For Call options, the Delta is given as a positive number between 0.0–1.0. In the example below, we see the Greeks for a Facebook Call option:

This fact tells you that the option's price will move up or down by 58.97% of the underlying stock price change. Or more simply, if the stock price were to rise by $1, the price of the option (for 100 shares) would rise by $58.97. Likewise, if the stock price dropped by 40 cents, the option would drop by $23.59, 58.97% of $40.

Delta is influenced by all the factors that influence options pricing. The more in-the-money an option is, the larger Delta is going to be. For example, if an underlying stock has a share price of $223, and the strike price of a Call option is $222 with five days left to expiration, the Delta is 0.57, meaning that the price of the option will rise and fall by $57 for every $1 rise or fall in the underlying stock price. On the other hand, if the strike price is $210, with five days left to expiration, the Delta is 0.99, and so the option price will rise or fall by $99 for every $1 rise or fall in the underlying stock price.

The longer there is to expiration, the lower Delta is. That is because the underlying stock price is less influential when there is a long time to expiration—because an option has more of its price tied up in extrinsic value (specifically in time value). Using the above example, a $210 strike price and a $223 share price, with 30 days to expiration Delta, is 0.83. So rather than moving by $99 with a $1 change in underlying stock price, the option price would only move by $83, meaning that the stock price is about 19% less influential when there is more time for this particular option to expiration date. In all cases, the underlying stock price will be less influential when there is more time to expiration, but it will not be 19%. It will be some other value.

Delta is one of the most important of the Greeks that options traders keep an eye on. The following one is Theta.

Theta

This Greek is a quantifiable measure of time decay. It will give you an idea of how much your option will decline in value the following market open. Each day when markets open, options held overnight lose value automatically due to time decay. Since this represents a decline in value, Theta is listed as a negative number. For example, if we have an option with a strike price of $225 and the underlying share price is $221 with ten days to expiration, Theta is -0.15 for both the Call and the Put option, which are priced at $176 and $574, respectively. The following day at the market open, the Call and Put options' prices will immediately drop to $161 and $559.

Theta is going to change with time, but it changes slowly. The following day Theta increases a bit, moving to -0.158 for the Call option and -0.157. This explanation will help you understand how much value your option will lose with each passing day.

Of course, like anything else, the example we've used to illustrate this holds everything else constant so that we can focus on Theta and how it describes what happens to options prices. At the market open, however, prices of shares are going to be very actively moving. Suppose that the share price increases to $222.50. When the underlying share price changes, Theta will change as well. And it turns out that the underlying share price has more influence on Theta than the passage of a single day. So, while the passage of time increased Theta a little bit, raising the share price by $1.50 increases Theta to about -0.17 for both the Call and the Put. If the share price rose, even more, to say $225 a share, Theta for the Call would increase to -0.181, while Theta for the Put would rise to -0.179. Of course, this would have more impact on the options' price than on Theta, but it is important to know what happens to Theta as share prices move.

Vega

The implied volatility of an option can have a pretty significant impact on options prices. Higher implied volatility will increase options prices, and options traders often prefer higher levels of implied volatility. Since this is one of the crucial factors determining an option's price, a Greek is called Vega. Keep in mind that Vega has the same value for Call and Put options with the same strike price and expiration date.

Vega is a decimal value that will tell you how sensitive the options price is to a 1% change in the implied volatility. To see how it works, like anything else with options, it helps look at concrete examples.

Let's return to our example of a stock trading at $302 a share. Like some of the other parameters we've looked at, Vega is at the highest value when the strike price is equal to the share price, that is, for an at-the-money option. The further the strike price is away from the share price, and the smaller Vega will be. The impact is fairly large. Let's illustrate this with an implied volatility of 5% (chosen small so we can study the difference of large implied volatility in a minute).

If the strike price is $302 for an at-the-money situation, Vega will be 0.141. A Call and a Put will be priced at $71 and $70 in this situation if there are five days to expiration. If the implied volatility went up a single percentage point to 6%, the Call and the Put would both increase in value to $85 and $84, respectively. So, you can see that they increased in value roughly by $14. So, we can take Vega's value and multiply by 100 to see how many dollars the value of an option would increase (or decrease) by for every one percentage point change in implied volatility.

Increasing the volatility while holding everything else the same doesn't have a very high impact. Vega doesn't change at all under that scenario. With a strike price of $302 and 5 days to expiration, Vega is the same if the implied volatility is 5% and 18%. The implied volatility could be any value between 1-100%, and Vega would remain 0.141. It starts decreasing if implied volatility goes over 100%, which is possible but extremely rare.

What about the expiration date? The further you are from the expiration date, the higher Vega is. At one year from expiration, Vega would be 1.193. So that would mean a 1% change in implied volatility could mean a $119.30 increase in the price of an option, all other things being equal.

This fact should make the light bulbs go off in your head. In situations where you expect implied volatility to increase—such as an approaching earnings call—you can make big profits on options that are far from the expiration date. This fact works especially well with LEAPS and works when you are a month to six weeks or so to expiration. At 30 days to expiration, Vega is 0.345, meaning that a 1% rise in implied volatility will lead to a $34.50 increase in the option price. Implied volatility can go up by huge margins as the earnings call approach, so this can give you a good opportunity to earn profits. You can buy Call and Put options on a stock a month before an earnings call and watch as implied volatility increases and adds to your options' prices, generating profits.

Rho

The final Greek that we need to take note of is Rho, but it's not that significant in today's environment compared to the others. Rho is a measure of the sensitivity of options prices to changes in interest rates. Specifically, it is based on a somewhat hypothetical "risk-free" interest rate generally taken to be the interest rate on a ten-year U.S. Treasury. If the interest rate goes up by a large amount, Call options will rise in value, and Put options will decrease in value. If interest rates drop, Put options will increase in value, and Call options will decrease. Rho is generally pretty small; a typical value might be around 0.06 for a Call option and -0.06 for a Put option. The value of Rho tells you how much a one percentage point change in the risk-free interest rate is going to impact the price of the option. Generally speaking, it's not very important to worry about. In the late 1970s, interest rates rose rapidly to very high values, so in that kind of environment (or one in which interest rates were rapidly decreasing), it might be significant. But in today's environment, it is not something that you should worry about or base your trading and investment decisions on.

Minor Greeks

That is our summary of the major Greeks. Other Greeks are called the minor Greeks. These go by Color, Epsilon, Lambda, Speed, Ultima, Vera, Vomma, and Zomma. These are more obscure and can be used by large professional traders that have sophisticated computer models. Still, these extra Greeks are not worth worrying about (even Rho is not worth worrying about, and Gamma is even a bit questionable to devote attention to). For most traders, Delta, Theta, and Vega give you all the information you need to know to have a solid foundation for managing your trades.

CHAPTER 12:

How to Find the Ideal Broker

When it comes to selecting brokers, you have many options available. There are full service, discount, online, etc. Understanding the differences between them and selecting the ones best suited for your purposes is crucial if you wish to succeed. Another area that many beginners ignore and then receive a harsh lesson in is the regulations surrounding options trading.

There aren't too many rules to comply with, but they do have significant consequences for your capital and risk strategies. This part is going to fill you in on all the details.

Choosing a Broker

Generally speaking, there are two major varieties of brokers: discount and full service. A lot of full-service brokers have discount arms these days, so that you will see some overlap. Full service refers to an organization where brokerage is just a part of a larger financial supermarket.

The broker might offer you other investment solutions, estate planning strategies, and so on. They'll also have an in-house research wing that will send you reports to help you trade better. In addition to this, they'll also have phone support if you have any questions or wish to place an order.

Once you develop a good relationship with them, a full-service broker will become a good organization to network with. Every broker loves a profitable customer since it helps with marketing. A full-service broker will have good relationships in the industry, and if you have specific needs, they can put you in touch with the right people.

The price of all this service is that you pay higher commissions than average. It is up to you to see whether this is a good price for you to pay. As such, you don't need to sign up with a full-service broker to trade successfully. Order matching is electronically done, so it's not as if a person on the floor can get you a better price these days. Therefore, a full-service house may not give you better execution.

Discount brokers, on the other hand, are all about focus. They help you trade, and that is it. At least not intentionally from a business perspective, they will not provide advice, and phone ordering is nonexistent. That doesn't mean customer service is reduced, far from it.

Commissions will be lower as well, far lower than what you can expect to pay at a full-service house. The downside of a discount brokerage is that you're not going to receive any special product recommendations or solutions outside of your speculative activities. Many people prefer to trade (using a separate account) with the broker they have their retirement accounts with, so everything is kept in-house.

So, which one should you choose? Well, if you aim to keep costs as low as possible, then select a discount broker. Only in the case where you're keen on keeping things in one place should you choose a full-service broker. These days, there's no difference between the two options otherwise.

An exception here is if you have a large amount of capital, north of half a million dollars. In such cases, a full-service broker will be cheaper because of their volume-based commission offers. You'll pay the same rate or as close to what a discount broker would charge you, and you get all the additional services. Whatever additional amounts you need to invest can be handled by the firm through their business wealth management line. You must understand a few terms, no matter which broker you choose, so let's look at these now.

Margin

Margin refers to the number of assets you currently hold in your account. Your assets are cash and positions. As the market value of your positions fluctuates, so does the amount of margin you have. Margin is an important concept to grasp since it is at the core of your risk management discipline. When you open an account with your broker, you will have a choice to make. You can open either a cash or margin account. To trade options, you have to open a margin account. Briefly, a cash account does not include leverage within it, so all you can trade are stocks. There are no account minimums for a cash account, and even if they are, they're pretty minuscule. A margin account, on the other hand, is subject to very different rules. First, the minimum balances for a margin account are higher. Most brokers will impose a $10,000 minimum, and some will even increase this amount based on your trading style. The account minimum doesn't achieve anything by itself, but it acts as a broker's commission.

The thinking is that with this much money on the line, the person trading will be a bit more serious about it and won't blow it away. If only it worked like that. Anyway, the minimum balance is a hard and fast rule. Another rule you should be aware of is the Pattern Day Trader (PDT) designation.

PDT is a rule that comes directly from the SEC. Anyone who executes four or more orders within five days is classified as a PDT ("Pattern Day Trader," 2019). Once this tag is slapped onto you, your broker will ask you to post at least $25,000 in the margin as a minimum balance. Again, this minimum balance doesn't do anything but the SEC figures that if you do screw up, this gives you enough of a buffer.

Will the strategies in this manuscript get you classified as a PDT? Well, this depends on you. Each strategy by itself plays out over a month or more, so once you enter, all you need to do is monitor it, and if you want, you can adjust it. However, if you're going to avoid the PDT, you're limited to entering just three positions per workweek.

My advice is to study the strategies and to start slowly. Trade just one instrument at first and see how it goes and then expand once you gain more confidence. At that point, you'll have enough experience to figure out how much capital you need. Remember that even exiting a position is considered a trade, so PDT doesn't refer to trade entry.

Margin Call

One other aspect of margin you must understand is the margin call. This message is dreaded for most traders, including institutional ones. The purpose of all risk management is to keep you as far away as possible from this ever happening to you. A margin call is issued when you have inadequate funds in your account to cover its requirements.

Remember that your margin is the combination of the cash you hold plus the value of your positions. If you have $1000 in cash, but your position is currently in a loss of -$900, you'll receive a margin call to post more cash to cover the potential loss you're headed for. You'll receive it well in advance. If you don't post more margin, your broker has the right to close out your positions and recover whatever cash they can to stop their risk limits from being triggered.

The threshold beyond which your broker will issue a margin call is called the maintenance margin. Usually, you need to maintain 25% of your initial position value (that is when you enter a position) as cash in your account. Most brokers have a handy indicator that tells you how close you are to the limit.

The leading cause of margin calls is leverage. With a margin account, you can borrow money from your broker and use that to boost your returns. Let's look at an example: if you trade with $10,000 of your own money and borrow $20,000 from your broker to enter a position, you control $30,000 worth of the position. Let's say this position makes a gain of $10,000 to bring its total value to $40,000.

You've just made a 100% return on this investment (since you invested just $10,000) despite the total return on the position is 33% (10,000/30,000). What happens if you lose $10,000 on the position, though? Well, you just lost 100% despite the position losing only 33%. Leverage is a double-edged sword.

It is far too simplistic to call leverage bad or good. It is what it is. If you're a beginner, you should not be borrowing money to trade under any circumstances. When you're experienced, you can choose to do so as much as you want. Please note that I'm differentiating between the leverage you borrow money and the sort of leverage options you provide. A single contract gives you control over a larger pie of stock with options, but the option premium still needs to be paid. It is, therefore, cheaper to trade options than the common stock. If you were to borrow money to pay for the option premium, then you're indulging in foolish behavior, and you need to step away.

There's a difference between leverage being inherent within the instrument's structure and leverage to increase the amount of something you can buy. The latter should be avoided when you're a beginner.

Execution

A favorite pastime of unsuccessful traders is to complain about execution. Their losses are always the broker's fault, and if it weren't for the greedy brokers, they'd be rolling in the dough, diving in and out of it like Scrooge McDuck. Complaining about your execution will get you nothing. A big reason for these complaints is that most beginner traders don't realize that the price they see on the screen is not the same as what is being traded on the exchange. We live in an era of high-frequency trading, and the markets' smallest measurement of time has gone from seconds to microseconds. Trades are constantly pouring in, and the matching engine is always finding suitable sellers for buyers. Given the market's pace, it is important to understand that it is humanly impossible to figure out an instrument's exact price.

Therefore, within your risk management plan, you must make allowance for high volatility times when the fluctuations will be bigger. For now, I want you to understand that just because the price you received was different from what was on screen doesn't mean the broker is incompetent.

How do you identify an incompetent broker? Customer service and the quality of the trading terminal they give you access to are the best indicators. Your broker is not in the game to trade against you or fleece you. Admittedly, this is not the case with FX, but we're not deliberating FX in this manual. So, stop blaming your broker and look at your systems instead, assuming the broker passes basic due diligence.

CHAPTER 13:

Binary Options Trading

Binary options are similar to traditional options in many ways except that they ultimately boil down to a basic yes or no question. Instead of worrying about what exact price an underlying stock will have, a binary option only cares if it will be above one price at the time of its expiration. Traders then make their trades based on if they believe the answer is yes or no, at which time it will be worth either $0 or $100. While it may seem simple on its face, it is important that you fully understand how binary options work, as well as the time frames and markets they work with. It is also important to understand the specific advantages and disadvantages that they have and which companies are legally allowed to offer binary options for trade.

It is important to keep in mind that binary options are a derivative created by their association with an underlying asset, which means they don't give you ownership of that asset in any way. As such, you would be unable to exercise them as a means of generating dividends or utilizing voting rights.

The Benefits of Picking Binary Options

- **The potential for a high return:** This form of investing is risky, but if you learn to read the market properly, you will find that it has a lot of potential for a lot of money to come to you. If you do well with this trading option, you could see a return on investment between 60 to 90 percent.

- **The risk is fixed:** You will know right at the beginning how much money you stand to lose or to win depending on which way the prediction goes, which helps make it easier to decide on your choices. Other investments can end up being a lot of guesswork, and if things go south, you can lose a lot more than you put into the whole thing. On the other hand, with binary options, you know exactly how much you stand to gain and lose right off the top.

- **You can even win after losing:** Since you will find that the risks on these options are high, some brokers offer a return on money that you invested if your predictions were wrong. It will not be the full amount, but getting a small percentage of your money back can be encouraging compared to losing it all.

- **Easy trading:** These are easier to trade on. Other stock market options make this hard, but the platforms for binary options help the investor trade without hassle. You can work with a live chat feature to do this or even with your broker if you have some questions. Besides, there are only two options for most of your trading options, making things easier.

- **Rewards:** The risk associated with any binary option will always cap out at the initial trade cost because the worst result for any option is for it to time out and be worth $0. The reward is also capped and based on the amount of the initial investment. As an example, if you purchase a $20 binary option, then you are always going to make $100 at most, which means you will make $80 and have a 4:1 risk/reward ratio, which is better than you will find in most other situations most of the time.

However, this will only be in your benefit for a limited time, as gains will never increase or pass $100 regardless of how much movement an underlying asset may have.

The easiest way to mitigate this particular downside is to double down on options contracts from the start simply.

How to Trade Binary Options

Binary options are currently traded on the Nadex exchange, which was the first exchange created expressly to sell binary options in the United States. It offers market access and its trading platform, which always has access to the most current binary options pricing.

It is also possible to trade options on the Chicago Board Options Exchange, which can be accessed by those with options trading approved brokerage account through more traditional means. When doing so, it is important to keep in mind that not all brokers will offer options trading, which means that if this is a route you are considering going down, you will need to plan accordingly and choose your broker with these services in mind.

Trading via Nadex costs 90 cents per trade with a maximum of $9 per transaction; this means that lots greater than 10 are essentially free. The fee is not deducted from the trading account until the trade has expired, and if the trade does not end profitably, then there is no charge. Trading on the Chicago Board is subject to standard brokerage fees.

Choose the right market. Nothing is stopping you from trading across various asset classes at once when it comes to binary options, and, indeed, Nadex allows trading across most of the major indices, including the S&P 500, Nasdaq 100, Russell 2000, and the Dow 30.

Available global indices include those from the UK, Germany, and Japan. Trades are also available for a variety of forex pairs.

Another popular option through Nadex is binary commodity options, including crude oil, natural gas, gold, copper, silver, corn, and soybeans. There are also several options for trading based on a specific news event, which means you can buy options on similar things.

Binary Option Timeframes

Weekly Trading

Weekly binary options are listings that allow trading in the short-term and lots of opportunities to hedge the choices you make. As you might infer from the name, weekly trading means working with options that expire in exactly one week, with the standard being for them to be listed on Thursday and expire the next Friday. While this type of binary options trading has been around for quite some time, they were largely only used by investors who followed the cash indices. This exclusivity has changed in the past decade as the Chicago Board has started expanding this type of trading practice. So far, there are nearly 1,000 opportunities to do so each week.

Beyond just having a specific timeframe, weekly binary options are different from more traditional options. They can only be secured 21 days out of the month, so they aren't listed as expiring in the monthly style. In the week that monthly options are set to expire, they are technically classified as weekly options.

The biggest benefit of this type of binary option is that it makes it extremely easier to purchase what you are exactly looking for in a specific trade without needing to come up with additional capital to end up with more than you need. For those interested in selling, weekly binary options make it easier to do so more regularly instead of waiting a month or more between sales.

Weekly binary options trades are also worth considering in that they ultimately lead to lower costs for trades with larger spreads like Calendar or Diagonal spreads, as you can sell weekly binary options against them in the interim. They also come in handy when it comes to higher trading volumes, especially in hedging larger positions in risky markets. Likewise, if the market is range-bound, the weekly market will still be fruitful thanks to strategies like the Iron Condor or Iron Butterfly.

The biggest downside to weekly binary options is that you won't have much of a chance of things changing in your favor if you choose poorly from the start. Likewise, if you are looking to shorten the binary option in question, it is important to keep in mind that it would only take a relatively small overall move to push something into the money.

As you will have less time to turn a profit when dealing with weekly binary options when you do make a move, it is vital that your timing is as precise as possible as if you choose poorly. Then you can easily find yourself paying for something that will end up being worthless as soon as you put your money down. It is also important to consider how much risk the option offers, as buying in bulk is always cheaper if you have the data to back it up.

Along similar lines, it is important to avoid naked puts or calls when trading in the weekly timeframe as these often end up with a lower probability of success overall. If you are quite specific regarding your chosen trades' directions, then a structured trade or a debit spread may be a better choice.

Selling weekly at a reliable pace for the long-term can lead to reliable profits when done correctly. It is likely only to work out if you strive to define your profits from the start, which means you always need to know the odds on all of your current options to avoid selling yourself short by mistake. Selling weekly makes it easier to secure reliable profits while requiring extra margin to prevent unmitigated losses if you end up choosing poorly.

It is important to talk about the most reliable type of trades to move forward within this scenario and look into trades with lots of implied volatility. It is more likely to work out in your favor in the long run due to the nature of binary options. Spreads are another useful way to make money from the weekly market. The overall implied volatility will typically be higher than the monthly variation, which means the spread can help deal with an unexpected change in direction with the speed required to do something about it. Meanwhile, selling against a long option will decrease the amount of volatility in the transaction, which means the ideal point to use the debit spread will be near the current price, assuming the ratio of risk to reward is close to 1 to 1.

CHAPTER 14:

Trading with LEAPS

The acronym LEAPS stands for Long-term Equity Anticipation Securities. They are a type of option with expiration dates that are longer than normal. They last for at least one year and sometimes go as far as three years into the future. As mentioned earlier, the expiration dates of options are typically a few months into the future. The typical option expiration ranges are three months, six months, and nine months. That's because options are typically a short-term way of investing.

LEAPS step away from the norm and have a longer shelf-life compared to your average option. They still possess the qualities as a normal option. LEAPS appeal to investors that want a long-term investment without being obliged by that investment. It also appeals to the investor who is anticipating a profitable yield from a particular market in the future but does not have the capital at hand to make that substantial investment. They are more affordable than such assets like stocks because they are still options and thus stick to option price ranges despite the long expiration date. LEAPS normally have a slightly higher price than other short-term contracts.

LEAPS has a seat at the options table because sometimes the associated asset's value needs more time to appreciate. Typical options expire in a few months. These options can yield profits in a short amount of time, but there is also the risk that the transaction might not be as profitable if the stock or other associated asset does not move significantly up or down.

LEAPS are the solution that allows the time for appreciation of the associated asset. A trader can extend the expiration on that LEAP option with another LEAP if the time is still too short for the asset to reach profitability. For example, a LEAP with an expiration date of 2 years can be held for one year then be sold and replaced with a 3-year expiration date. This is called rolled LEAPS.

Rolling the option forward is normally relatively inexpensive because it still carries the same characteristics. Other factors can become unpredictable, though. Such factors include interest rates, dividends, and volatility.

The question that stumps many traders about LEAPS is whether to use a Call option or a Put option. The answer to that is dependent on whether the trader expects a bullish or bearish price movement. If the trader believes that the associated asset is bullish by the expiration date, he or she should buy Call options. If instead, he or she believes that the associated asset will drop in value by the expiration date, then the trader should buy Put options.

Best Strategies for Using LEAPs

Some strategies work best when it pertains to LEAPS, and this list includes:

- **Long Call:** This involves purchasing LEAPS Call options to anticipate a long-term bullish trend in the market.

- **Long Put:** This involves the purchase of LEAPS Put options in anticipation of a long-term bearish trend in the market.

- **Rolling LEAPS options:** As mentioned earlier, this involves selling the LEAPS before the expiration date while buying LEAPS with similar characteristics with at least 2-year expiration dates at the same time.

- **The Bull Call Spread:** This options strategy is considered to reduce the initial cost of buying a Call option. This can help offset the higher cost of LEAPS compared to standard options. Only use this strategy if you are confident that there will be a moderate rise in the stock price to send it up to the strike price.

- **The Bullish Call Spread:** This is another strategy meant to offset the higher cost of LEAPs. It is a bearish strategy. Profits are earned when the stock prices fall.

- **Calendar Call Spread:** This strategy is meant for a trader who wishes to benefit from the associated assets staying stagnant in the market while also benefiting from the long-term Call position if the stock becomes more valuable in the future.

Benefits of LEAPS

LEAPS have several benefits, and they include:

- LEAPS are sustainable as they allow a trader to piggyback off-market trends. This possibility allows the trader to observe the movement of stock prices and have an option to buy or sell without making the full commitment of ownership.

- LEAPS are less volatile and so offer greater security. A trader who enters into such an option is looking at a stock increasing or decreasing in price over the long haul. This condition allows the trader the time to ponder on the profitability of pursuing the asset. This person can use data offered over that time, such as the current trends, news, and terms, to base their future decision.

- LEAPS can serve great security in your financial portfolio and provide shareholders with a greater grip of the stock.

- LEAPS allow time for improvisation because the expiration date is longer.

- Buying LEAPS is cheaper than buying several standard options back-to-back.

Disadvantages of LEAPS

There are two sides to every coin. So, just as LEAPS are beneficial, there are also a few downsides. The first disadvantage of LEAPS is the strike price. Because they are priced higher, the trader needs to see movement in the asset price to profit and take longer for the option holder to breakeven.

The longer expiration dates on LEAPS make them less predictable. Therefore, setting the price correctly so that a return is seen without the transaction being too costly can be difficult. Lastly, the trader will not benefit from any attached dividends or stock repurchases.

LEAPS are also sensitive to implied volatility and so can lower in value when implied volatility drops.

Tips for Getting the Most Out of LEAPS

- Pretend as if you are investing. This condition allows you to search for assets that you are interested in and maybe already have some know-how about. It makes it a lot easier to keep up-to-date with market trends than if you do not know anything about the asset and are not interested in learning more.

- Make use of the long expiration date. The long expiration date benefits have been stated, so ensure that these work to your benefit.

- Choose LEAPS that are more liquid.

- Prepare for the fact that LEAPS are more volatile than stocks but less volatile than standard options.

- Set targets for the stock prices compared to your LEAPS; knowing those targets will allow the trader to sell at the most profitable time.

- Have an exit strategy in case the option is not working out according to plan.

- Always be aware of your position and be prepared to leverage it. Even though the expiration date is far off, you need to keep abreast of whether the market is playing out as you anticipated. You need to be aware of the fluctuations in the asset's price. It will allow you to decide what makes this transaction the most profitable it can be for you. You can implement strategies like rolling the option forward and selling the first option as a loss so that you can move to another strike price that benefits you more.

Summary

LEAPS stands for Long-term Equity Anticipation Securities. It is an option that has an expiration date that is at least one year, which is a deviation away from the standard short options that carry expiration dates that are only a few months. LEAPS are a great option for a long-term investor who wants to experiment with options without being apprehensive about the financial market's volatility in the short term. LEAPS are also a great way for investors who do not have a great amount of capital available to them at present to enter into the market with lowered risk.

This long-term maturity has many benefits, such as being sustainable, more secure, and not subject to time decay. However, there are disadvantages, like the option being higher priced than standard options, being less predictable because of the far-off timeline, and taking longer to breakeven than a standard option.

To get the most out of trading LEAPS, the trader needs to be strategic. Tips like staying abreast of market trends despite having a longer expiration date, having an exit plan if things go left field, and be prepared to leverage your position will help the trader gain maximum profit.

CHAPTER 15:

Most Common False Steps in Options Trading

t is advisable for new trader options to learn various strategies and build on strong returns over time. There are also various things you should keep in mind before you start trading options. Some mistakes can be made, but if you're patient and avoid the pitfalls, you're going to succeed.

Don't Start by Buying Out-of-the-Money Call options

Many experienced stock traders who have switched to trading options also use this strategy: buy a Call option and wait to see if it can profit. It is close to the "*buy low, sell big*" stock market technique. Although it can provide good trading profits, this strategy does not reliably produce profits in trading options. In the long run, a dealer with options can lose a lot of money. Also, he may discover that he's not learning anything new.

An out-of-the-money option is a cheap investment since it depends on the chance to hit or pass the strike price. In most instances, the likelihood is tiny. The price of the option is, therefore, also poor.

Instead, a new options trader can write & sell an out-of-the-money Call option on the underlying asset that he/she currently owns. When a Call option is sold, the option for the writer has to sell the asset. Due to this duty, the writer will make a profit from the choice. If the investor is optimistic about the asset, he/she may make some money-ready to sell the stock, even as the price rises before the option expires. Don't buy right away, but instead sell and write Call options to make a profit.

Observe the Timing

In stock trading, it seems impossible to predict how the stock price will move. The same is true for selling options. A lot of times, fluctuation can happen overnight, before you even know about it. The options can skyrocket in price, and that's why you need to watch for any changes in the market.

In general, a trader must correctly forecast the course of price movements. They might not be correct at first, but seeing the difference would save you so many problems, and you'll know about where the trading options are going as a result of that. However, he/she must also foresee when the price will shift in the anticipated direction.

If a trader with a Call option makes a mistake in one or both of the criteria, he/she will take a loss on the premium paid. If the underlying asset takes a long time to shift in the planned direction, the profit will decline as the expiry date approaches. That's why you should know where this will happen and the estimated timing of the stock route's life. See where it's going to go, and from there, you can decide where you're going to end up as a result of this move.

Attempt Covered Calls

There is nothing risky about selling options using the call strategy in question.

The risk lies in the ownership of the underlying asset; the investor can lose a sum equal to the difference between the underlying asset's prevailing market price and the option's premium.

In most cases, the loss will be substantial. In writing and selling the option, there is no capital risk. There is a chance of opportunity, however, since the investor has a small upside. The purchaser can exercise the option when the price of the underlying asset soars. As such, the seller is losing future income. On the other hand, since the seller holds the underlying asset, the asset's price would have risen to the option's selling price.

In the flat market, the writer/seller retains a long position when earning the option premium. If the writer wants to go out after the asset price has gone down, he/she will simply buy back the option to close the short place. The writer will sell the underlying asset to close the long place. By closing the role, he/she can experience losses. The sale of Covered Calls is a low-risk and smart strategy for new option traders. An option trader can use it as he/she becomes more familiar with the trading of options.

Don't Use an All-Purpose Approach for Any Business Situation

Flexibility in options trading enables traders and investors to participate in trading under any market conditions. They will do this if they attempt to learn other techniques. They can buy spreads on different market conditions.

However, there is currently a strong business condition for using it. A Long Spread position has two options: selling a lower-cost option and purchasing a higher-cost option. These options vary only in the price of the strike. A Long Call Spread is a bullish stance (thinking the asset's price will rise), while a long-term spread is bearish (thinking the asset's price will fall).

In trading a spread, the time downside of one option can be a time advantage of the other. Therefore, the timing dilemma is compensated by spreads.

The downside of spreads, however, is that the investor has little upside potential. Not a lot of people make big spread profits. However, the possible loss is also minimal.

Strategies that could be "all-purpose" may seem like a smart idea, but sometimes doing that can obscure an investment's true potential. You could make more of one form of investment than another. Many people don't know this at first, but that's because they end up seeing that they missed an opportunity. Try calling for appropriate circumstances, and know what you should do in each case.

The Middle Men Involved

Investors and traders must be vigilant to distribute the trade. For traders, spread trading will cost many commissions because this kind of trading includes different trades. In the calculation for profit/loss, fees must be included in the equation. Finally, they need to know the dangers of deals with commissioners, who would claim a share of the income. Often a commissioner's net loss can be up to 30%, which is a lot if you look at how much you put in as a premium. Don't depend on intermediaries to make a profit. You can find cheap broker sites online, but make sure they are a legitimate place to use because sometimes there are bogus broker sites out there, and that may mean an even greater loss of money as a result.

Have an Escape Plan Before the Option Ends

Emotions have no position in the trading of options. To be successful, traders and investors must have a strategy and commit to executing it. A successful exit strategy has upside and downside exits; it also has time frames for each exit. Getting a strategy sets out good trading trends and encourages people not to think about it.

The trader of new options must know the amount of profit that will offer enough satisfaction. The trader must also know the amount of loss that he or she is prepared to bear. The trader must also know all sums in advance. When the benefit is achieved, the place must be cleared. The same goes for the downside goal.

Don't "*Double-Up*" To Restore Past Losses

In most cases, traders also find themselves in violation of their laws. In the case of stock trading, it could be possible to double up to recover losses. If the price is low, a stock investor will buy more shares. However, this may not be applicable in the trading of options.

Options are distinct from stocks. Thus, "*double-up*" doesn't make sense in the trading of options. Time decay must always be taken into account. Leveraging is possible in the trading of options. However, it may also cause the trader to lose heavily. To prevent a tragedy, it is necessary to minimize losses and close the place.

Be Vigilant About Trading Illiquid Options

The liquid market is perfect for options traders because it is easy to trade when active sellers and buyers are in position all the time. It also means that the next transaction is carried out at a price that is the same as the last.

The stock market has more liquidity than the options market because it provides more choices than the former. An investor who prefers to trade illiquid options can pay a higher price than the normal cost of options.

In general, it is prudent to exchange open-interest options at a minimum of 40 times the number of future contracts that one wishes to trade. For example, if an investor wants to exchange ten lots, the investor's liquidity should be at least 400 contracts. It's better to work with liquid options.

Don't Waste a Lot of Time Trying to Buy Back the Short Options

The options trader must always be prepared to buy back short options. Most of the time, the trader cannot determine early because he/she does not like paying commissions. The trader may think that the contract would expire without being exercised by the purchaser.

Finally, the trader might be hoping to make even a little profit from the deal. It's easier to buy back a short choice than to bear the risk of being out-of-the-money. In general, if there is still at least 80 percent of the benefit from the initial option sale, the investor must buy back the short option. Failure to do so would result in losses.

Dividend Payout Dates and Earnings Should Be Included in the Options Strategy

An options trader must track the dividend dates and earnings of the underlying asset. Option owners are not permitted to take advantage of dividends. If a large dividend has been declared, they will exercise a Call option to purchase the underlying asset-and, thus, collect dividends.

While the early assignment is difficult to monitor since it is very unpredictable, traders should detect imminent dividends not to be allocated early.

Also, the earnings season raises the price of options contracts. Any news about the underlying asset could increase the volatility of the asset. Trade options are notified after the announcement of earnings has already passed.

Pending dividends would raise the probability of assignment. Any investor who still wants to trade options with an accrued dividend must learn about the ex-dividend rate.

So, the earnings season raises the price of options and the volatility of options. Any trader who still wants to trade options in the course of this season may want to spread by going long on an option and going short on another one. The price of the underlying asset is normally inflated during the earnings season. As such, investors should expect that option premiums will also be inflated.

CHAPTER 16:

Technical Analysis

Professional traders often use a set of tools known as technical analysis to help them make their trades better. Specifically, technical analysis can help you detect developing trend reversals in stock charts. This information can help you get into and out of your trades at best possible time. Technical analysis is a favorite tool of day and swing traders, and some options traders use it, but not all options traders do. Nonetheless, you should have some familiarity with it to determine if something you feel could help your trading.

Technical analysis involves a wide range of tools. These include looking at moving averages and specialized types of charts known as candlestick charts. Some traders also look for stock chart patterns that can signify a trend reversal or change in price momentum.

It's important not to get too enamored with technical analysis. That is, you don't want to get into a mindset where you view technical analysis as "fact" because the cold truth about technical analysis is that it is a tool and nothing more. It is too easy to put far too much faith into technical analysis that isn't deserved. Nonetheless, technical analysis is a useful tool, and you can pick and choose specific tools of the trade that you feel will help you make more educated trading decisions.

Studying Trends with Moving Averages

The most important thing on a stock chart that a trader will look for is a trend reversal. If you are looking to profit from Call options, then what you will look for is a relatively low stock price or a stock price in decline, and then wait for it to show signs of a reversal. In other words, this is going to help you buy low and sell high. Once you have entered a position, the technique is to study the charts looking for the coming reversal once the price has peaked to exit your position.

Moving averages are the easiest tools to use for this purpose. A moving average takes several periods of stock data, and at each point, it calculates the average out to a fixed number of points. The definition of a "point" is up to the individual trader; it could be an hour, four hours, a day, or a week. It could even be five-minute intervals. If you plan on trading an option over 30 days, you will probably be looking at using days for your time frame. In that case, a 9-

period moving average would calculate the average of the closing price at each day, using the past nine days to do the calculation.

To spot trend reversals, traders rely on moving averages with different periods (but they will use the same definition of the period, be it a day, week, or five minutes). So, you could use a 9-period moving average and a 20-period moving average. Alternatively, you might use a 50-period moving average and a 200-period moving average.

A longer-period moving average will give you more information on the stock's historical pricing level in question. Different types of moving averages are going to treat this in different ways. A simple moving average will do a standard mathematical average of all data points. So, if we had a 9-period simple moving average for closing prices of Apple, on a particular day, it might calculate:

SMA = (212.41 + 213.11 + 212.50 +214.29 + 215.72 +216.01 + 217.22 + 217.50 + 216.95)/9

Many traders are completely content to use the simple moving average, but if you look at how it's calculated, you should note that all prices are treated the same. This measure is objectionable because if you are looking to make a trade, recent prices will be more important than older prices. We certainly want information from the stock's historical pricing level, but more recent prices will have the most impact on our trading decisions. For this reason, many traders use weighted moving averages that give more weight to recent closing prices and less weight to closing prices in the past. Two very popular weighted moving averages are used, the Hull moving average and the more popular exponential moving average.

To detect a trend reversal, you will use two moving averages on your stock chart of the same type but with different period lengths. So, you can use nine days exponential moving average with 20 days exponential moving average. No matter what type you choose and what periods you use, there are only two rules you need to worry about.

The first rule is known as a "*golden cross*". It happens when the short-period moving average curve crosses above the long-period moving average curve. It tells you that the stock is likely to be entering an upward trend. In the example below, a 50-day simple moving average and a 200-day simple moving average are used. Notice that after the golden cross (the 50-day moving average crossing above the 200-day moving average), the stock enters a relatively long-term upward trend.

This tool's beauty is that it is very simple to use—it is also something that a beginning trader can understand quite easily.

Of course, stocks are not always going up; otherwise, everyone would be rich. So, we have to know how to spot the development of a downward trend in prices. It's a so-called "*death cross*". In a death cross, the short-period moving average curve crosses below the long-period moving average curve.

It is clearly illustrated in the chart below, which shows a death cross for Facebook and the drop in stock prices that followed:

The question now is how to use crosses of moving average curves with options trading. You should see from the examples that it's quite simple. When you are looking to get into a trade, you should add the appropriate moving averages to your charts and then use a golden cross or a death cross as a signal to enter or exit trades.

For Call options, you want to enter a trade when there is a golden cross. Then, when the chart shows a death cross, exit your positions. It's that simple.

For Put options, you will do the opposite. That is, you will wait to enter your trade until you see a death cross. For options traders, since you can profit, either way, a "*death*" cross is also a signal for profits, but with using Put options. Then you hold your position until you've reached a level of profit you are comfortable with, or you see a golden cross, indicating a coming trend reversal.

Remember that with options, the expiration date and time decay are always lurking in the background, so you don't necessarily want to wait for another crossing to occur before exiting your positions. Each case will have to be evaluated individually.

Momentum

One of the most important concepts that stock traders look for is momentum. Price momentum occurs when many traders are either buying or selling a stock, pushing prices strongly in one direction or another. The tool you can use to study the momentum of a stock price is called the Relative Strength Indicator. You can add this to your stock charts to help you study the best times to get into and out of positions to maximize possible profits.

The relative strength indicator will be displayed below your stock chart. It is a curve that can go between 0 to 100. Typically, the values 0-30 and 70-100 are what traders are looking for on the chart. When the curve goes into the range of 0-30, this means that a stock is "*oversold*." That is, traders have sold off too many shares, pushing prices down to a level that makes it likely that new traders will now find the stock an attractive buy, so they are likely to start loading up on the stock and pushing prices upward again. The lower the RSI gets, the stronger this signal is.

On the other hand, if the RSI goes into the range of 70 and above, this indicates overbought conditions. In this case, frantic purchasing of the shares has pushed prices up too high, and traders are likely to start getting out of the stock because they want to get out before the price drops when there is a large selloff.

The RSI should not be taken in isolation. A good way to use it is to use it in conjunction with the moving averages. So, if you see oversold conditions with the RSI, together with a golden cross, that indicates that stock prices are likely to start moving upwards. On the other hand, if the RSI indicates overbought conditions, and you also see a death cross, this can be taken to indicate that stock prices are likely to be pushed in a downward direction soon.

An example chart with the RSI is shown below.

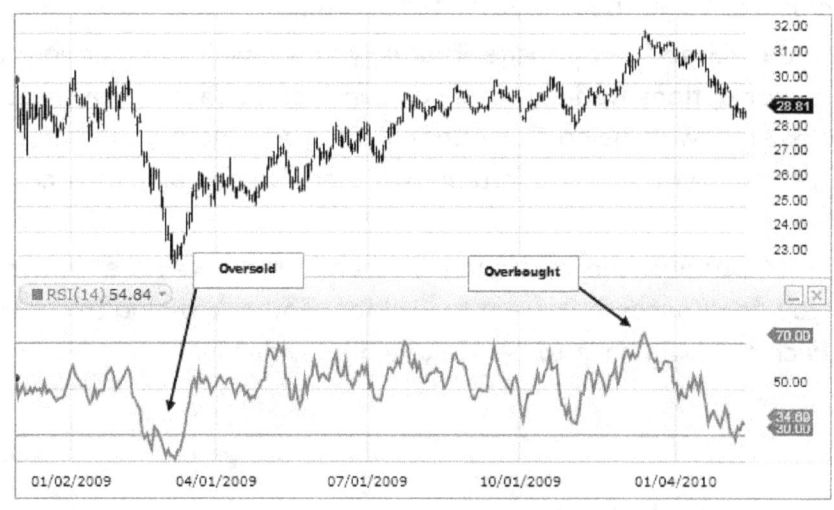

Support and Resistance

The concepts of support and resistance are important for options traders to understand, especially if you are interested in trading Iron Condors. These concepts are not complicated, so most readers will have no problem grasping them.

In many cases, a stock is not going to be shooting up or crashing to the floor. In fact, over most periods of the stock market, stocks will be bouncing around in the same price range, and possibly gradually increasing or maybe decreasing, but over relatively short periods staying the same. When this happens, we say that the stock is "*ranging*." The values that the stock prices range between are called support and resistance.

Support is the low-price level. So, while the stock is ranging, it will dip down to the support price level but not go below it. After it drops to support, it will probably start rising again. You want to look for a price that the stock reaches at least twice over the time frame you are looking to declare a support price.

Resistance is the upper price level that the stock cannot break above. Again, you want to look for the stock price to move up to the resistance price at least twice over the time frame. So, while the stock is ranging, it will drop down to support, then bounce around, go up to resistance, drop back down to support, and keep repeating this process. Stocks can do this for extended periods. For options traders, when the price drops to resistance, this is a time for those trading Call options to enter their positions. Put option traders would sell their positions at this point.

CHAPTER 17:

Strangles and Straddles

Strangles and Straddles are options strategies that allow the investor to benefit whether the stock price goes up or down. They carry similarities such as buying an equal number of Call options (options that give the trader the right to buy the stock) and Put options (options that give the trader the right to sell the stock), the same asset both have the same expiration date.

The difference lies in the number of strike prices. The Strangle has two different strike prices, while the Straddle has one common strike price.

These two strategies are called volatile strategies because, unlike many strategies that bet on whether options are bullish or bearish, these strategies bet on the financial market's volatility.

Types of Volatility

There are five different types of volatility as it relates to financial markets. The first one is known as price volatility. Price volatility describes how the prices of assets move up or down. This type of volatility is affected by the supply and demand of that asset. There are external factors that affect supply and demand. Prices may rise up and down due to the season. For example, prices may fluctuate due to whether or not it is summer or winter in the tourism industry. This factor fluctuates because of demand. Weather is another factor that can affect price volatility. For example, the agricultural sector's financial markets fluctuate due to the supply of certain crops at certain times of the year in certain regions. Emotions are also something that causes price volatility. For example, gas prices continue to be high because of emotional attachment on its huge demand.

Stocks are also highly volatile. This characteristic is called stock volatility, and this unpredictable nature is what makes stock a risky investment. Even though the returns on investing in stock can be quite high, the losses can be disastrous as well. That's why there is a science to picking stocks that are likely to be profitable. Investors use the measurement known as a Beta to predict stock volatility.

Covariance is a measure of a stock's sensitivity relative to that of the financial market, while variance is a measure of how the market moves relative to its mean.

Another type of volatility is historical volatility, which is how a stock has performed over the last 12 months. If a stock's prices varied wildly over that period, it is very volatile and, therefore, risky to invest in. If a stock was less volatile over that period, it becomes more attractive to invest in. However, an investor may choose to hold onto the stock for a longer period to achieve greater returns. To gain maximum profitability, the trader will study the market to see when it is the best time to sell the stock at the highest value. This technique is called "*timing the market*", and as such, this technique does not work with volatile stocks because they are unpredictable.

Implied volatility is a measure of how a stock will perform in the future. It is an opinion as there is no guarantee of what will happen in the future. Generating this opinion depends on certain factors that can be accounted for in the present. These factors include:

- The price of the stock
- The market price of the option
- The expiry date of the option
- The interest rate
- The strike prices
- Dividends

While implied volatility in no way evaluates stock, it does evaluate how options should be prepared for selling and buying. It helps develop a fair price for the option to be profitable even if the stock price goes down. An option's price sensitivity concerning implied volatility is known as Vega. This figure represents the amount that an option price will change in reaction to a 1% change in the stock's implied volatility.

Vega is also one of the Greeks. These are a collection of indexes that measure an option's sensitivity concerning other factors. Other measures include Delta, Gamma, and Theta. Delta describes the option's sensitivity concerning the price of the stock. Theta describes an option's sensitivity concerning how time affects the premium of an option. Gamma is a reflection of the rate of change of the Delta.

Other Greeks include:

- Lambda. It is the one that describes an option's sensitivity concerning the associated asset's value.
- Rho, this is the one that describes an option's sensitivity to the interest rate.

The last type of volatility is known as market volatility, and it describes the rate at which prices change on any financial market. All of these types of volatility affect how an options trader will utilize strangles and straddles strategies.

Now we will look at the benefits and risks of each of these strategies below.

The Strangle Strategy

This strategy is employed when the trader strongly believes that the stock price will move either up or down but still protect himself if he is wrong. There are both long and short strangles.

The Short Strangle

Also called a sell strangle, this is a neutral options trading strategy. The trader sells:

- 1 out-of-the-money Put
- 1 out-of-the-money Call

Both of these will have the same associated stock and the same expiration date. It is a tactic employed when the trader thinks that the stock will be relatively stable on the market in the short term. Profit is gained when the stock prices on the expiration date are between the options' strike prices. This profit is limited. The formula for this profit is calculated like this:

Premium Received - Commissions Paid = Profit

Unfortunately, the risk of this type of option is unlimited. Loss is experienced if the price of the stock goes up or down sharply by the expiration date.

With a Call option, this is calculated this way:

Price of Stock - Strike Price of Short Call - Premium Received = Loss

The loss with the Put option is calculated with this formula:

Strike Price of Short Put - Price of Stock - Net Premium Received + Commissions Paid = Loss

There are two break-even points with such a transaction. When calculated on the Short Call, the formula is this:

Strike Price of Short Call + premium Received = Break-even

The formula for the Short Put break-even point looks like this:

Strike Price of Short Put - Premium Received = Break-even

The Long Strangle

It is also called the Buy Strangle, and it is based in a neutral position in options trading. The trader buys:

- 1 out-of-the-money Put
- 1 out-of-the-money Call

Both of these will have the same associated stock and the same expiration date.

It is a strategy used when a trader believes that there will be great volatility in the market. This strategy's beauty minimizes the risk of loss and introduces the potential for unlimited profit. This profit is gain when the price of the stock takes a sharp move up or down. The formula for the Call option is:

Price of stock - Strike Price of Long Call - Premium Paid = Profit

The formula for the Put option is this:

Strike Price of Long Put - Price of Stock - Premium Paid = Profit

The risk of this type of strategy is that if the stock prices are trading between the strike prices of the options bought on the expiration date. Both options will become worthless.

Net loss is calculated with this formula:

Premium Paid + Commissions Paid = Loss

The trader can break-even at 2 points with this strategy. The formula for break-even on the Call option is:

Strike Price of Long Call + premium Paid = Breakeven

The formula for break-even on the Put option is:

Strike Price of Long Put - Premium Paid = Breakeven

The Straddle Strategy

With this options trading strategy, the trader protects himself regardless of whether the stock's price moves up or down. Think of it as someone straddling a fence. This person can jump to either side of the fence to ensure the situation benefits him or her. There are both long and short straddles.

The Short Straddle

It is also called a Sell Straddle, as well as a naked straddle sale. This neutral options strategy work by the trader selling:

- One at-the-money Call

- One at-the-money Put

The options have the same associated stock, strike price, and expiration date.

These types of transactions have a limited profit, just like a short strangle. The profit is achieved when the stock price trades at the options' strike price on the expiration date. The formula for calculating this is:

Net premium Received - Commissions Paid = Profit

The risk is unlimited and is incurred when the stock prices move higher up or down by the expiration date. On the Call option, the formula for calculating this is:

Price of Underlying - Strike Price of Short Call - Net Premium Received = Loss

For calculating the loss on the Put option, this formula is used:

Strike Price of Short Put - Price of Stock - Net Premium Received + Commissions Paid = Loss

This strategy also has two break-even points. When calculating the break-even on the Call, it looks like this:

Strike Price of Short Call + Premium Received = Breakeven

Calculating the break-even on the put looks like this:

Strike Price of Short Put - Premium Received = Breakeven

The Long Straddle

Also known as the buy straddle, this strategy is a neutral one whereby the trader buys:

- One at-the-money Call
- One at-the-money Put

This strategy ensures that both options have the same associated stock, strike price, and expiration date.

The profits associated with this strategy are unlimited. Because the trader has long positions on both the Call and Put options, profits grow when the stock prices move up or down strong enough. Profit is calculated with the following formulas:

Price of Stock - Strike Price of Long Call - Net Premium Paid = Profit

Strike Price of Long Put - Price of Stock - Net Premium Paid = Profit

Another benefit of using this strategy is that the risks are limited as the loss is incurred when the stock price trades at the strike price on the expiration date. Loss is calculated with this formula:

Premium Paid + Commissions Paid = Loss

Like all of the strategies mentioned above, break-even for Long Straddle is calculated at 2 points. The formulas for calculating this as follows:

Strike Price of Long Call + Net Premium Paid = Breakeven

Strike Price of Long Put - Net Premium Paid = Breakeven

CHAPTER 18:

Basic Options Trading Strategies

Options trading requires knowledge of different strategy types, which you need to learn if you want to be proficient in this trade. Here are the time-proven strategies being employed by veteran options traders.

Long Call

The Long Call option strategy gives you the chance to decide whether an underlying stock's strike price will go up or stay. This strategy will allow you to gain profit without the risks associated with outright stock ownership. And since Call options cost less than buying the stock itself, you can leverage even more shares than you could than with the stock.

However, care should be taken when purchasing short-term Calls that are "out-of-the-money." As a new trader, they may seem attractive because of the inherent cheap price, but you may end up losing your hard-earned investment. Keep in mind the life span of Call options is somewhat limited, and there is always the possibility that the stock price will never go beyond the strike price just in time to gain profits, so the option may end up losing its value.

Profit and Breakeven Profile

Maximum Investment Loss = Net Price of Premium Paid

A Long Call strategy's maximum gain is unlimited because of the possibility that the stock will continue to gain more value over time.

A Long Call's break-even is computed by adding the strike price's premium. If a particular stock trades at $100 and you want to purchase a Call option for a 110-strike price at $2.00, the break-even value will be $112.00.

Sample Scenario

Let's say stock ABC trades at $100 a share, and you bought a Call option for a 100-strike price valued at $10. Since there is a contract controlling 100 shares, you will need to pay $1000 (100 multiplied by $10).

You are betting that the price of the underlying stock will go above $100 by $10 at the very least in hopes of gaining profit from the transaction. For each dollar that the stock price goes above its strike price, which is after the initial $10 rise, you will realize a profit of $100 from the option, and this can be lucrative if the stock's price keeps on climbing.

On the other hand, if the stock price remains at $100 per share, or worse, dives lower than its strike price, this option will be worthless by its expiration, and you would have lost $10, which is a hundred percent of your investment.

To conclude, a Long Call is a strategy that will make you bet on the stock price's increase. You must be prepared for the possibility of losing the entire investment if you are wrong. Although there is potential to earn higher through the Call option than buying the stocks outright, there is also a greater risk.

Long Put

This strategy gives you selling rights for an underlying stock at a set price. When you purchase a Put option, you wager that the underlying stock will fall lower than the strike price before the option expires. You are reducing the risk because instead of shorting the stock, you use a Put option.

If the stock price rises, the shares' delivery is not required as you lose only the option's cost instead of losing more as the stock price keeps on climbing. In this scenario, the Put option will expire worthlessly. You have to be careful, especially with short-term puts. Also, buying many Put options will increase your risks since each of these contracts might expire worthless, with you ending up losing your entire investment.

Buying Put options

There are different reasons you should purchase Put option contracts, and some of these can be speculative, which means you are wagering that the price of a stock will fall early. A Long-out option is also referred to as a protective Put because you can use it as a hedge stock against those you already own, and it protects your stock from sudden loss or turnaround in value.

For example, when your stock price suddenly dives, an increase in value can be realized by getting a Put option since it will offset the losses you may incur from the sudden change in the stock's value.

Short the Stock or Buy a Put

If you want to impose a more bearish position in trading, there are two popular strategies that you may adopt—shorting the stock or buying a Put option.

Shorting the stock can be pretty risky, considering that a stock price can go up infinitely, so the risk associated with this strategy is also unlimited. Buying a Put option is the better alternative since you can lose only the Put option's cost, limiting the risk. Both are shorting the stock and buying a Put have limited potential for profit as the gain's value as the stock's price falls. The big difference is that the stock's price can fall until it reaches zero value, but with a Put option, you can capitalize on the stock's downward movement while limiting the risk to the premium you paid for the options contract.

Profit and Breakeven Profile

Maximum Investment Loss = Net Price of Premium Paid

The Long-Put strategy's maximum gain is unlimited since the stock's price can continue going down, so you get more value over time until the prices reach zero.

Breakeven for Long Put options can be computed by deducting the premium paid from the strike price. If a stock trades at $100 and bought a Put option for a 90-strike price at $2.00, you will break-even by $88.00.

Sample Scenario

For example, stock ABC trades at $100, and you believe its price is heading down, you may purchase a $2 Put option with a 90-strike price. If the stock dives to $85, you would have gained $5 on your 90 Put option, but since you bought it for $2, your net gain is $3. If the stock price catches up, never reaching $90 or below, you would have lost your $2 investment. The Long-Put strategy allows you to bet on a stock price's decline. You should be prepared to lose your entire investment if you bet wrong. As the price of the underlying stock goes down, you earn more via a Put option than short-selling since the risks to the latter are uncapped as there are no limits to how much the stock price will rise over time.

Short Call

A Short Call is also called a Naked or Uncovered Call. It's defined as selling the Call option without considering the underlying stock. A Short Call is not an option strategy recommended for beginning option traders. The risk for this strategy is high, and profits are limited. You only gain benefits from the premium you'll get when you sell the Call option.

Short calls are typically made when underlying asset prediction is bearish or neutral. After you make the sale, you must sell the underlying stock at its strike price. It's in your interest with a Short Call if all the Call option's value will be lost when it expires. When following this strategy, it's better to wait for the strike to price to go "out-of-the-money" by one standard deviation meaning the strike price has gone below the strike price. But keep in mind that the strike price can affect the premium you'll receive. With the Short Call strategy, you also want a decrease in the implied volatility since there will be a corresponding decrease in the sold option's price. So, if you choose to close before it expires, it will cost you less than high implied volatility. Remember that you can take advantage of the decreasing time before expiration in the short call strategy. When you close by expiration, you will benefit if the sold option's price is decreasing.

Profit and Breakeven Profile

The maximum gain for the Short Call strategy is equal to the net premium. The Short Call strategy's maximum loss is unlimited because the stock price can move continuously and without end.

The Short Call option's break-even can be computed by adding the premium you get from the strike price to the original price. If a stock trades at $100 and bought a Call option for a 110-strike price at $2.00, you will break-even by $112.00.

Sample Scenario

For example, stock ABC trades at $100, and you want to sell a Put option with a 110-strike price, you will gain a $2 premium by doing so. If the stock reaches $115, you must purchase it at $1115 and then sell it to your call buyer for $110, causing you to lose $5. But since you also received $2 as a premium, your net loss will be $3. However, if the stock price continues to go down, never reaching $110, you will keep the premium of $2 as profit.

Aside from individual stocks, you may also sell what are called Call index options. The reason for trading them is because of their lower volatility compared to stocks. If a stock's price stayed below its strike price, a Short Call's profit potential is low. Theoretically, the risk for this strategy has no limit if the stock price keeps rising. You might want to sell calls since the profit potential can be high if an option is considered too "out-of-the-money."

Short Put

A Short Put option practice means you are wagering that the stock price will go up or stay as is until the contract expires. If the put expires as "out-of-the-money," or more than the strike price, you get to keep the entire premium.

As the Short Put seller, you are forced to buy the stock at its strike price if your buyer chooses to exercise the option.

A Short Put can be a very useful strategy since it gives you increased income by receiving premiums from other investors who wagered that the stock price would fall. Hence, if you use the short put strategy, you get the premium and protect yourself when the market is flat or there is very little movement. Then again, you need to sell your puts sparingly since you are obligated to buy the shares if the stock goes lower than strike-price when the contract expires.

Short Puts can be used to get better purchasing prices on stocks that are overpriced by selling these Puts at much lower strike prices, where you would choose to purchase the stock.

Profit and Breakeven Profile

The maximum profit gain from the short Put option strategy is equal to the net premium received. The maximum loss is unlimited in this strategy because the stock price can change against your expectations until the value reaches zero.

CHAPTER 19:

Tips for Success

If you are interested in embarking on the journey of earning money through options trading, there are a few issues to address before getting on board. Here are some of them:

Know When to Go off the Manuscript

While sticking to your plan, even when your emotions tell you to ignore it, is the mark of a successful trader, this in no way means that you must blindly follow your plan 100 percent of the time. Without a doubt, you will find yourself in a situation from time to time where your plan is going to be rendered completely useless by something outside of your control.

You need to be aware enough of your plan's weaknesses and the changing market conditions to know when following your predetermined course of action will lead to failure instead of success. Knowing when the situation is changing versus when your emotions are trying to hold sway will come with practice, but even being aware of the disparity is a huge step in the right direction.

Avoid Trades That Are Out-of-the-money

While there are a few strategies out there that make it a point of picking up options currently out-of-the-money, you can rest assured that they are most certainly the exception, not the rule. Remember, the options market is not like the traditional stock market, which means that even if you are trading options based on underlying stocks buying low and selling high is not a viable strategy.

Suppose a Call has dropped out-of-the-money. In that case, there is generally less than a 10 percent chance that it will return to acceptable levels before it expires, which means that if you purchase these types of options, what you are doing is a little better than gambling. You can find ways to gamble with odds in your favor of much higher than 10 percent.

Never Get Started Without a Clear Plan for Entry and Exit

More important than setting entry and exit points is using them, even when there is still the appearance of money on the table. One of the biggest hurdles that new options traders need to get over is the idea that you need to wring every last cent out of every successful trade. The fact is that, as long as you have a good trading plan, there will always be more profitable trades in the future. It means that instead of worrying about a small extra profit, you should be more concerned with protecting the profit that the trade has already netted you. While you may occasionally make some extra profit ignoring this advice, odds are you will lose far more than you gain as profits peak unexpectedly and begin dropping again before you can effectively pull the trigger.

Read

It is really important, at least one book or article per week. It will teach you a lot of things, especially the secrets. It will also provide you with a deeper understanding of the risks and rewards involved.

Trade for Income, Not Wealth

If you do this thinking that you will be getting returns at 120%, you should reconsider. While one or two investments may yield such returns, the vast majority of options will not.

Start with Enough Capital

One of the first things that you need to make sure of is that you are set up with enough capital to get into the investment. Capital is the amount of money you can place into your account to help pay for any of the transactions you choose, and that can be used if you end up experiencing a loss while you are trading.

You should always leave a little bit of money in your trading account. This condition will help you out when you are in the middle of a trade and make it easier for your broker to keep working on trades without worrying about a delay while your fund's transfer.

Avoid the Big Risks

Good option traders don't like a ton of risk, and they don't understand why they should take a big gamble so that they can get a tiny chance at a big payday. Rather than going after things like this, they will work on some high gain trades but lower risk.

Be Sure to Diversify

Diversification is of the utmost importance. Having a not adequately diversified portfolio is a rookie mistake; however, many professional investors prefer not to diversify because of how money is run in the United States.

Try Not to Panic

People do not make money from panicking in stressful situations. You will always encounter better times to leave or make a move rather than moves brought about by nervousness or panic. This one is the downfall of many people interested in investing but it can't master the craft.

See the Positive About It and Find Opportunities

The next time you notice a situation with trading that has brought much panic, you should immediately take the opposing side. Some of the best trades you make can involve the trade having been cleared out from people panicking and using their market orders without understanding that the doors for exiting are not as large as they believe or assume.

It doesn't mean all of the merchandise people leave out of panic is worth investing in over long periods. Usually, when the market or stocks get socked, there will be a bounce-back that lets you leave in a better position than you would have if you went along with what everyone else was doing when they left too fast.

Trade at the Right Times

Since you will learn how to avoid big risks when you are an options trader, you will learn how to be very careful about your timing when entering and exiting the market. You have to read the market the right way to learn the best time to do both of those tasks. These investors have spent their time doing a lot of research, and they know how to look at the big picture, rather than always calling up the broker and hoping that they can trust that person.

Learn How to Be Focused

A few people believe that options trading is super easy, and then they jump in and become overwhelmed by what they are dealing with. If you are not used to this kind of investment, it may seem a bit hard to deal with initially.

If you find that you are a person who is not able to focus on the task that you need to easily, then it is easy to have trouble with options trading because you are missing out on a lot of things. A trader who can maintain their focus for a long time is more likely to get more out of this trading style.

Never Follow the Crowd

One of the worst things that you can do is try to follow the crowd and hope that will work out well for you. Many beginners find it easy to look to the experts for advice, and then they will exactly follow what that expert says without doing any of their research or trusting their own judgment.

There is nothing wrong with getting advice from an expert, but your plan will not be the same as theirs.

You are the only one who has an idea of your limits and goals, and while you can listen to the advice that others give you, it is important to think for yourself and pick out a plan that works for you.

Keep It as Simple as Possible

Options trading is a tough market by definition. You do not need to perplex things any further. Keep your strategies as simple as possible, use the simplest technical analysis tools, and manage your money in the simplest way possible. The rest will fall into place on its own.

Do Not Overtrade

When you start dealing with inexpensive options, it will be very easy to lose track of your trading. Keep the number of contracts at a manageable level.

Pay Attention to Rankings

Especially if you are dealing with spreads and particularly if you are a novice, qualification rankings are available to consult at all times. An option that is not ranked high is not a good option, and it will probably cost you money.

Be Consistent

Before you ever make any trade, you will want to have a clear idea of the strengths and weaknesses of the various stocks in question and the best point to enter into a trade, and at what point you are going to want to exit the trade. If things go poorly, and also where you will exit if things ultimately go as well as you could expect. Once you have made a plan, it is important to stick with it even if your emotions make a compelling argument for going in another direction instead. It is important to always trust in your plan as it was made during a period when you were thinking as rationally as possible. Giving in to your emotions at this point is akin to gambling with your investments.

Keep the Mood of the Market in Mind at All Times

Fundamental and technical analysis is all well and good. Still, the two will only take you so far before you run into instances where the market seems to balk at the logical choice and move off in an unexpected direction. It typically happens when the market's will goes against the status quo thanks to an unexpected outpouring of support from traders thinking with their guts instead of their brains. The best way to go about doing this is to keep tabs on what the major players in your market of choice are up to, as this will typically act as a litmus test for the feelings of the market as a whole.

Keep a Trading Journal

While it might seem to be a waste of time at first, the fact of the matter is that keeping a journal of all of the trades you make can be an extremely effective way to analyze what you are doing right, as well as what you are doing wrong when it comes to options trading. While one type of analysis or the other might pique your interest when it comes to trading at the moment, keeping a trading journal will allow you to look at your trading results from a more analytical perspective once you have gotten a little more distance and perspective on what it is that you are doing.

CHAPTER 20:

Sector Analysis

Fundamental analysis will be an analysis of hard data on a financial instrument, commodity, or company. Some of the data that are going to be collected will include:

- Total revenue
- The earnings per share
- The price to earnings ratio
- The leverage or the amount of debt to equity
- The product pipeline or the future potential growth driver
- The advantages the company may have compared to other competitors
- Conditions that could favor or disadvantage the company in their sector or their industry
- Peer to peer comparisons
- Hot sector manias
- Short interest
- The regulatory environment and pending changes
- The way that the company is managed

These can be important when working on fundamental analysis, but it isn't a complete list. These include the most common options and help you figure out how well a company is doing and why it will go either up or down shortly.

Since there are so many different factors to consider with fundamental analysis, these factors will be the most important. These factors help you figure out whether the company is a good investment for your needs.

Total Revenue

The first factor that we are going to consider is the total revenue of the company. This revenue number will measure the total sales of a company for their products and their services. It can be a good indicator of whether the company is doing well or not. If the revenue is growing at a steady pace one year after another, the company is doing well. If the revenue numbers drop from one year to the next or stay flat, it shows that the company is having some trouble growing and that the profits are not meeting where they should. As a swing trader, you want to check whether the stocks you want to purchase are growing or declining in revenue and see if that will align with the trades you want to do. If they don't, then you need to look at what other options are available for you.

Earnings Per Share

The earnings will be calculated when you take the total revenue and subtract the production's direct costs. You want to find positive earnings in the long-term because this means that the business will keep operating. Earnings and profits are not the same things, though. Profits are calculated by subtracting the additional costs of doing business, such as interest paid on debt. At some point, the company needs to turn a profit, or investors will lose patience, leaving the company. The long-term value of the company, to keep it simple, will be based on the future cash that the company can generate by doing business. The more it is expected to generate in cash in the future, the more investors will value it today. Like with the total revenue, companies' stock prices will usually rise if there is an expected growth in EPS numbers.

Price-to-Earnings Ratio

The price-to-earnings ratio, also known as P/E, is considered a fundamental way to measure the stock and how its price movement is going. This P/E will give you a view of how the market is pricing the shares concerning what it is earning. It will be calculated by taking the company's price per share and dividing it by the earnings per share. Similar to the ratio that we used for EPS, you can use this information to determine if the company's stock is undervalued or overvalued by the marketplace. You do this by taking the P/E of stock and comparing it to the industry's other companies.

Debt to Equity

Most companies will need some funds to start up and operate the business. They need some money to pay their employees, money to help them purchase inventory, money to help them buy all the office supplies and equipment, etc. The money they use to do this will come from their equity or by taking on more debt. Debt will be borrowed money that the company will use to help them operate but usually cost them interest. The debt has to be repaid at one point or another.

On the other hand, equity can be the money that is invested in the company, and the investor will be given shares in return. Those shares are going to represent some percentage of ownership in that company. The investor hopes to sell the shares later on to earn a profit or hold onto the shares and earn dividend payments. Debt and equity are going to represent different levels of risk for a company and its shareholders. Debts will come with obligations to pay interest and to repay any outstanding loans at some point. It means that the debt is going to present a higher risk to the company when it is compared to the equity. Equity doesn't have any obligations with it. Still, it carries a risk for the shareholders because if the company doesn't do well, the debt holders will get whatever is valuable. The shareholders will potentially get nothing. When you are trying to look at how the company is doing financially, it is good to balance equity and debt. Generally speaking, you don't want a company to have more debt than equity. More debt with a company will be risky for the company and can hinder how well it will do in the future. A little debt isn't a bad thing, but you want to make sure that the company can handle that debt. Depending on what the company is doing, you will find that there are times when the company may take on more debt. If they are expanding or putting more money into research and development, the company may put in more debt to help with these. These are still good signs that the company is a good investment and doing well. If the company is taking on more debt to do regular operations or having trouble paying off their debts, this could be a sign of big trouble.

Return on Equity

The return on equity will measure how much profit a company can generate with the money that the shareholders invested in the company. It is going to be expressed by a percentage. For example, if an investor puts $100 into a savings account and can earn 1% a year on it, they should have $101 after a year. Similarly, investors for a company will expect to see the company they chose to make a good return on investment. The ROE measure will indicate how well the company is doing in terms of the invested capital. Companies with a higher ROE and look to be growing will be held higher by the investors. Searching for higher ROE companies will be another option you can experiment with as a swing trader when you set the scanner. The companies with good ROE or who promise higher ROE soon will be seen as valuable and can be good ones to invest in as swing trader. These are just a few of the different things you can look at when doing a company's fundamental analysis. It is usually not the only strategy that a swing trader will use because it doesn't rely on any charts like the other methods. Still, it can certainly give you a good idea of how a stock is doing, how well the company is managing itself, and how it can help you determine if that is a great investment to make at that time.

Company Fundamentals

When swing trading, all the focus seems to be on all these indicators to show us where the market will go. Nevertheless, you need to keep in the back of your mind that you are not a day trader, and you should even be willing to go for a long time (relatively speaking) on your trades. That might be several months, but always less than a year. However, unlike day traders, we need to keep in mind that the company fundamentals are important for swing traders to study. Keeping up with company operation details will help you be well placed to profit from swing trades timed with earnings calls or release a new product.

Financial Statements

To properly assess the value of a company's stock, you will need to have a solid handle on its finances. That doesn't mean you need to become an accountant, but before entering a large trade on a company's stock, you should have a look at all of its financial statements. It turns out that swing trading will overlap with the type of analysis someone like Warren Buffett would do when buying a stock. Knowing whether a stock's current price is over-or undervalued is an important starting point before making bets on future swings in the price.

To get enough information to make informed swing trades, you don't have to go to a great extent in studying this information. Most of this information is available on sites like Yahoo Finance. The information you need will be under a tab labeled Financials after you select a particular stock. There, you will find three things to look at—the income statement, balance sheet, and cash flow.

Yahoo Finance lets you view the information on an annual basis or quarterly. First, let us familiarize ourselves with what we can find inside each report.

Income Statement

The income statement can give you a plethora of information about the health of the company. It will include revenue, gross profit, operating expenses, income from continuing operations, and net income. You'll want to keep your eye on viewing the income statement to look at the annual values and see how they are changing with time. Did the company experience growth over the past five years? Is the growth continuous, or is this a company in decline?

CHAPTER 21:

Selling Options

Selling options is a strategy that is used to generate regular income. Selling options is a little simpler but carries a higher risk.

Selling Covered Calls

If you have 100 or more shares of a particular stock, you can sell covered calls against your shares. People can use a common strategy to earn money off their shares, but you always face the risk that your shares will be called away if the option is exercised. One strategy that can be used is to sell out-of-the-money calls when you don't expect the share price to rise to the Call option's strike price over the contract's lifetime.

For example, Facebook is trading at $190.25 a share. You can sell a $210 call for $0.64, so for all 100 shares, one option contract would net you $64. It is for an expiration date of 30 days. Or you could take a higher level of risk and sell a $195 call for $4.05, which would give you a premium of $405 per option contract. If you had 500 shares, then you'd receive $2,025 in premiums. Not a bad passive income, and all you have to do is hope that the share price stays below the strike price.

If the share price closes in on the strike price, then you will be faced with a dilemma—risk having the option exercised if the share price rises above the strike price, or you can buy back the option and cut into your profits. With a few days left to expiration, the option you sold may be worth $2.05, so you could buy back the five options you sold, and you'd reduce your net profit to $1,000.

You could go further out, even selling LEAPS. In that case, the premium paid is much larger. A Facebook LEAP with a $195 call that expires in 18 months has a premium of $30.58, so selling five contracts for your 500 shares could bring in an income of $15,290. Of course, there is a higher risk that the share price will rise above the strike price over 18 months than there is over the short term.

The one principle to keep in mind selling covered calls is that you could lose your shares if the option is exercised. With that in mind, you should only select a strike price that is of a higher amount than what you had paid for the shares. That way, if you are forced to sell the shares, then you are not taking a loss doing so. That can make losing the shares easier to deal with. So, if we had purchased our shares at $200 a share, we would not select a $195 strike price because that represents a potential loss, which would be given by the price we paid for the shares minus the strike price and then less the premium aid, in this case, $200 - $195 - $4.05 so we'd end up losing $0.95 on the trade. If you had purchased the shares at a lower price, say $190 a share, then the $195 strike would make sense since if the stock price rose and the shares were called away, we'd still profit by selling the shares.

Protected puts are the put version of a covered call. The risk with a protected put is that the shares will be "put to you," and you will have to buy the shares, so you will be required to have enough capital in your account to cover the purchase.

Of course, the trick to selling options is to pick a strike price where you think the option will expire worthlessly. There is always the risk that you're mistaken, but if you think the share price will rise for Facebook, to use an example, you could sell a protected $190 put for $4.95, earning $495 per contract. If the share price rises, the options will expire worthlessly, and you would keep the premium and profit from the deal.

Selling Naked Puts

Selling naked puts is a popular strategy for traders that are given level 4 status. If you can get this level from your broker, you can consider this possibly profitable strategy. Of course, the key is choosing the right strike price.

When a put is "naked," that means it isn't backed by anything. However, you are still required by law to fulfill your obligations should the option be exercised, but one way that traders avoid this problem is by buying the options back if there is a chance they would be exercised. The time value may work in your favor, which will make the options cheaper and so you can buy them back and still profit.

Another consideration is to choose a relatively low implied volatility, which reduces the chances that the stock will move much over the lifetime of the option. But that is a trade-off as well, as implied volatility that is a few points higher can result in a large increase in the premium received for selling the option.

Consider IBM. The stock price is at $139.20, but you could sell a 30 day $135 put for $2.44, or $244. You could even sell in-the-money puts. A $145 put would sell for $748 if you sold five contracts that would be a 30-day income of $3,640.

Selling in-the-money puts could be risky but beneficial if it was believed that IBM shares were set to rise in price. If the price rises above the strike price, then the options will expire worthlessly.

While it carries a higher risk since a long time to expiration, Selling LEAPS gives a higher probability that the option will move in the amount and allows you to sell at high premiums.

A $130 put for IBM expiring in 18 months would sell for $13.20, so selling five contracts would give you a premium of $6,600. Bid-Ask spreads can be large for LEAPS, and the volume is probably small. For this particular option, we find that the bid-ask spread is about 80 cents, which isn't too bad, meaning selling it might not be that difficult. Daily volume is small at 10, but the open interest is 1,282. Experienced traders often recommend an open interest of 500 or higher since that indicates enough people are buying the contracts.

The risk with naked puts is that you will be forced to buy the shares. Again, if it looks like that might turn out to be the case, you can buy the contracts back. Selling out-of-the-money options that expire in the near term can leave you in a better position since the options will probably expire worthlessly, and you will be able to keep the premium without having to buy back the options. If you have to buy the shares, the loss would be the share price minus the market price. But of course, you'd have to get the capital to buy the shares as well.

So, if you sold a Put option on IBM with a strike price of $138 expiring in 6 weeks, it would sell for $3.70. If the share price dropped to $136, you'd have to use cash to buy the shares at $138 and possibly lose $2 a share by selling them—or you could simply keep them and wait for the price to go back up. Plus, your loss would be offset by the premium, so your break-even point is the amount of the strike price minus the premium paid.

Selling Naked Calls

You can also sell naked calls. It means that you sell Call options without owning the shares of stock. The risk that the option will be exercised means that you would have to buy the shares at a higher market price and then sell them at the lower strike price. So, the key here would be to sell out-of-the-money calls at strike prices that you doubt the stock will reach over the option's lifetime. The same strategies can be used, and if it looks like the share price is rising, you can buy the options back to avoid being assigned.

Looking at IBM, some modest out-of-the-money Call options 30 days to expiration have good prices. A $141 call, which is almost $2 out-of-the-money, is $3.55, so selling one contract would give you $355.

Suppose the stock was trading at $195 a share. You could sell a call with a 45-day expiration with a strike price of $200 for $4.46 or $446. If we find that the share price has risen to $197 with ten days to expiration, the Calls would now be priced at $1.88 (totally $188). So, you could buy them back and still have a profit of $258 per contract, avoiding the risk that you would be assigned if the share price kept rising. Of course, at $3 out-of-the-money, you might wait. When the share price rises to $199 with seven days left, the calls would be $218, so you'd be cutting a little more into your profits. But if it dropped $1 the next day, then the Call option would only be worth $1.58.

Remember, when you sell options, you make money on the time premium. Or put another way, time decay is your friend. Out-of-the-money, options lose value rapidly as the expiration date approaches.

The biggest risk with selling naked Call options if you can't buy them back is having to buy the shares at a high price and then selling them at a loss to honor your obligations. Suppose that a stock is trading at $95 a share, and you sell a Call option that has a $100 strike price; If the stock breaks out and, say, rises to $130 a share, someone might exercise the option. Since you sold the call naked, you'd be forced to buy the shares at $130 and sell them at the $100 strike price, losing $30 a share, which would be partially offset by the premium, which might be around $1 per share.

So, selling naked calls can be profitable but carries a lot of risks as well. The key to successfully selling naked calls is picking the right strike price and choosing a stock that you don't believe will have price movements that are large enough to cause the option to be in-the-money.

Broker May Force Sale

Note that most brokerages may automatically exercise options that expire in-the-money. So, you will not want to let an option expire in-the-money unless you are prepared to buy or sell the shares as required.

CHAPTER 22:

Risk Management

The old saying that "*An ounce of prevention is like a pound of cure*" is applied to risk management. It is necessary to keep your losses minimal, and it is important to protect your investment capital because it is your freedom to invest. Warren Buffett was quoted as saying, "*Rule number one: never lose money. Rule number two: Never forget rule number one.*" With this in mind, you must handle risk.

If you want to win, you can't always play the offense. Playing defense is critical if you want to trade successfully over the long term. Here we will explain the risk management techniques that can help you in your company. This part stresses the importance of treating option trading as a company, and the second half discusses risk management techniques.

Manage It Like a Business

If you were managing a business, you would have to put together a business plan that involves trading strategies and comprehensive plans for conducting the business and managing expenses (before starting a business). You're expected to build the same attitude when trading options. Developing a strategy and working hard are the keys to your success.

You should have targeted profit targets, risk management plans, a trading philosophy that suits your strengths and personality, and the best trading resources at your disposal. Remember the Wall Street adage that "*The bulls make money, the bears make money, and the pigs are killed*".

Before entering into any option transaction, you should calculate your maximum benefit, maximum loss, break-even point, and success probability. You should build a view of the course, pacing, and magnitude of the underlying stock and have strategies readily available at your fingertips to put yourself in a position to optimize your return and reduce your losses. You should have an idea of the risks before trading options.

Have a Plan

What options strategies are best for you depends, in part, on the sum of your money, the risk tolerance, and the trust you have in deciding the course, timing, and magnitude of the various market movements. For example, if you are confident in your ability to predict course, timing, and magnitude, you may want to buy a Call or use bull and bear debit spread strategies. If you're uncomfortable being so reliable, you may want to sell the options.

Discipline and commitment are important factors that are key to your success. You're not allowed to let your feelings control your investment decisions. To trade successfully, you must create your own set of guidelines on when to buy and sell. Buying and selling options, like most investments, can be an emotional roller coaster if you let it go. You should trade when you are level-headed and cool, using a predetermined systematic strategy.

Establish Goals

In certain cases, a far-out-of-the-money option might be offered for what seems to be a small premium, but when you measure your return on an annualized basis, you might realize that your returns will be outstanding. The object is to replicate the sales cycle every month, every two months, or every fifth months to maximize returns over the year. Since you have short-term odds on your hand, you can be tempted to sell many options, but you should avoid the temptation because of the risks.

When selling an option, you can't make more money than you collect, but different techniques can be used to make your returns more appealing. For example, assume that you have a $100,000 account and sell five out-of-the-money S&P 500 futures with $1 spreads every month. In that scenario, you're going to collect $1,250 a month for those options, generating an annual return of $15,000. If you also write call spreads simultaneously, you'll receive an extra $1,250 a month. You would also increase your annual return to $30,000 a year or 30 percent compared to your account's $100,000 starting balance. If you add $2,000 in interest, your total return is $32,000, or 32 percent. Look at another way, if you believe that you can earn $2,000 in interest per year, then you'll only have to earn $8,000 in options over the year to get an outstanding $10,000 (10 percent) return. Of course, you're not going to be able to make a profit every month or every quarter, but I think you get the idea.

You should exit a position with a predetermined benefit or loss objective; for example, the rule of thumb might exit a trade if the loss is 50% of the sum paid. Another rule might be to profit and close a deal if you profit from more than 75% of the premium charged or received.

Developing an Edge

Average investors can find it difficult to compete with large funds that spend millions of dollars on research and access knowledgeable sources. However, in some ways, a small investor may have an advantage over large funds because it can enter and leave the market as opportunities grow and not be hampered by the requirements to be invested at all times.

Which options strategies are best for you depends, in part, on the amount of capital you have, your risk tolerance, and your level of confidence. When dealing, you should not sell to the point that you can't sleep at night. Much of the time, you're trading options, you should be trading conservatively, but there are other moments when you need to know when to put on a full-court press. It doesn't mean you're going to take undue risk, but there are times when you're supposed to be more heavily involved than others. Of course, there are periods when you should be totally out of the market. You can never feel like you are pressured to be on the market.

Understand More Than Just One Technique

One of the easiest ways to mitigate the risk is to become as informed as possible so that you know what you're doing. No options strategy works on all market conditions, so you need to learn a variety of strategies. It does not mean that you need to become an expert in any options strategy, but it does mean that you need to consider more than one strategy to succeed under various market conditions. For example, stock trading options are your best choice in some situations when you can see an individual business that you would like to trade. Still, trading in an ETF, index, or S&P 500 futures option may be to your advantage in other market conditions. That way, you can trade from one market to the other, depending on which market offers the best opportunities at the moment. Note that some excellent ETF advances provide traders with realistic ways to short markets and commodities for the first time.

The good news is that there are several ways to make money trading stocks. You may be attracted to buying a call or Put options because you want big profits at a relatively small price, or you may be attracted to selling options because you want odds on your side or stable returns. Therefore, you should try to align the way you trade options with your risk tolerance and investment style. It is up to each investor to decide their investment style and risk management profile. Unfortunately, there are just as many ways to lose money if you don't know what you're doing.

Open Standard Brokerage Accounts

You can open brokerage accounts to allow you to trade a host of different options and take advantage of the margin. You should understand how options trading can be influenced depending on whether your portfolio is a taxable account, an IRA, a standard brokerage account, or a futures account; you should also understand how to optimize interest income and reduce commissions and taxes.

Open accounts and which accounts to open can be confusing, as brokers vary in terms of software, trading options, futures, margins, and interest. Some brokers have advanced option software that allows you to join, exit, and evaluate complex options positions. You can find a broker that allows you to trade in futures options. Firms such as Thinkorswim and OptionsXpress are online trading firms dealing in options. They have one-click trading platforms that execute trades, evaluate options, and perform real-time position management. Some brokers only allow investors to trade conventional stock accounts, while others only allow investors to trade futures. Some brokers have a broad range of stock and investment services but a restricted range of futures trading. You can shop around and open at least one stock brokerage account and one futures account, making sure that both accounts allow you to trade options. You can contact many stock and futures brokers and open accounts that allow you to trade as freely as possible. As a result, you will be in a position to be versatile in terms of trade stocks and options without unnecessary constraints. By setting up accounts in the stock and futures markets, like the IRA, you will be able to make a profit as opportunities arise. If you don't open those accounts, you probably won't be able to take advantage of the opportunities they present themselves to you. Usually, the most restrictive type of account from a margin perspective is the equity IRA, and the least restrictive account is the standard futures account. Futures accounts typically provide a trader with greater flexibility in trading due to reduced margin requirements and short-term ability.

IRA

Margin trading is not allowed in the IRA, and some brokers do not allow options to be exchanged in such accounts. However, some equity brokers approve some defined-risk options transactions. There seems to be a broad difference in what is permitted between brokers, so you need to contact your broker to find out what kind of options trading you can do if any. If you are dissatisfied with your broker's response, consider transferring your account to another stock brokerage or opening a futures account. Some stock brokerages can allow options to be traded in an IRA based on an investor's suitability, given that trades are defined-risk transactions such as call-purchase, put-purchase, cash-secured writing, spreads, and covered calls. Unsecured (naked) call transactions are not allowed in the IRA, but a naked call transaction can be permitted if appropriate funds are available in the account. However, you might be able to trade a bare call or put an option on a future IRA account. If your capital is small, you can consider purchasing options in your IRA (which does not require a margin) and selling options outside of your IRA (which requires a margin).

Synthetic Strategies

Synthetic strategies are obscure and rarely used by small traders. To make a synthetic put, you must have a large margin account. To set it up, you will short the stock, so you will borrow shares of stock from the broker and sell them on the market, hoping to buy them back at a lower price. Then you will buy a Call option on the same stock. If the stock price rises, you will make a profit on the Call option to help offset the loss of having to buy the shares back at a higher price (if you borrow shares from the broker, you have to buy them back and return them to the broker at some point). If the stock price drops as expected, you will lose money on the Call option, which will expire worthlessly, but you will make the expected profit from shorting the stock. You can buy it back at the lower share price, return the shares to the broker, and then the profit from doing that less the cost of the Call option is your net profit. So, this involves shorting stock using a Call option as insurance.

Traders can find more highly flexible investing alternatives with options. There are so many strategies to recreate synthetic option positions.

These positions offer investors a plethora of ways to obtain their investment goals. Besides synthetic positions, options have many other alternatives. For instance, many investors work with brokers who charge a little margin for shorting stocks. Other traders work with them (brokers) who do not wish to short stocks. The incapability to do the downside when required limits traders and investors. However, no broker can rule against traders for buying puts to "*play the downside.*" It is a big benefit for investors. Options also allow traders to trade the "*third dimension*" of the market.

Interestingly, they can even trade-in "no direction," stock movements, and during volatility. Mostly, stocks do not show "big" moves; but investors have the edge to trade in stagnation. Thus, options can only offer multiple alternatives that can give them profit in all types of markets.

CHAPTER 23:

Advanced Concepts and Volatility

As an options trader, you need to learn about the variables that can affect an option's price and the ins and outs of implementing the right strategy. A stock trader who is familiar and good with predicting future stock price movement might think that shifting to options trading is easy, but it's not. There are three changing parameters that an options trader must deal with—the underlying stock's price, the time factor, and volatility. A change in any of these factors will affect the price of the option.

The price of an option is also called the premium, and the pricing is per share. The option seller receives the premium, which gives the buyer any right to the option. The buyer is the one paying the premium to the seller, and they can exercise this right or allow the option to expire without any worth in the end. The buyer is obliged to pay the premium whether the option is exercised or not, which means the seller will keep the premium, in the end, no matter what.

Let's have a simple example. A buyer paid a seller for purchasing rights to stock ABC for 100 shares and a strike price at $60. The contract expires on June 19. If the option position becomes profitable, the option will be exercised by the buyer. If it does not seem to bear profit, the buyer can just let the contract expire. The seller then keeps the premium.

There are two sides to the premium of an option—its intrinsic and time value. You can compute an option's intrinsic value by getting the difference between the strike price and the stock price. For the Call option, it is the stock price minus the strike price. For the Put option, it is the strike price minus the stock price.

To value an option, at least theoretically, you will need to consider multiple variables such as the underlying stock price, volatility, exercise price, time to expiration, and interest rate. These factors will provide you with a good estimate of the fair value of an option that you can incorporate into your strategy for maximum gains.

The value of Puts and Calls are affected by underlying stock price movements straightforwardly. That means when the price of a stock rises, there should be a corresponding rise in Call value as well since you can purchase the underlying stock at a reduced price compared to the market's, while there is a price decrease in Puts. Conversely, there should be an increase in the value of Put options when the stock price dives and a decrease in Call options since the holder of the Put option can sell the stock at above-market prices. This pre-set price you can sell or buy is called the option's strike price or its exercise price. If the option's strike price gives you the advantage of selling or buying the stock at a cost that gives you immediate profit, that option is considered "in-the-money."

Time

"Time is money". This adage still holds true and even applies to options trading. Thus, understanding how the Greek Theta works and how it affects the pricing of options is very important. If you still remember, the Greek letter Theta represents the effect of time decay on the value of an option. All options, Call or Put, lose their value as the contract expiration nears, but the value loss rate of an option contract is a function of the amount of time remaining before it expires.

The extrinsic part of the value of an option is the only factor affected by time decay. That means an option that's "in-the-money" will have the same intrinsic value until the contract expires. For example, if a stock trades at $3, a Call for a 30-strike price will retain its intrinsic value of $3 from the start until expiration. Still, any value that exceeds $3 is considered an extrinsic value and will be affected by the time decay.

However, Theta does change over time. Let's assume that a stock's price remains unchanged. A $2.75 "out-of-the-money" option with a -0.15 Theta will have a reduced value of $2.60 by the following day. The Theta then may only be set to -0.12, which means the option's cost will be down to $2.48 the next day if stock prices remain unchanged. The option's value will gradually approach zero while it's still "out-of-the-money."

You also have to remember that Theta's effect becomes more and more apparent as the expiration nears. You should anticipate a rapid acceleration of the time decay within the remaining few days before the contract expires.

Options that are "at-the-money" possess the highest value, extrinsically. That's why these options have their Thetas set to highest. Deep options "in-the-money" or "out-of-the-money" have their Thetas lower because compared to "at-the-money options," they have lower extrinsic values. And the less extrinsic value an option has, the less they will lose as time decays.

The only way for the Theta position to be positive is to have short options. It is because short option positions work best when the market is stable. Wide swings both up or down hurt option positions, and only time will help as it passes by. Other strategies also benefit from time's passage, such as neutral strategies, e.g., Long Butterfly. The less time there is before the contract expires, the less probability for the underlying stock to rise or go down and reach unprofitable territories.

There will always be a trade-off between market movement and time for every option position. It's impossible to benefit from the two at the same time. If time is helping your option position, it will be negatively affected by the price movement.

Volatility

Volatility affects most investment forms to some degree, and as an options trader, you should be familiar with this element and how it affects options pricing. By definition, volatility is the tendency of something to fluctuate or change significantly. In general investment, volatility refers to the rate a financial instrument price rises or falls.

A low volatility financial instrument has a relatively stable price. Conversely, a high volatility financial instrument is prone to dramatic price changes, either way. In general, financial market volatility can be broadly measured. So, when the market becomes difficult to predict and prices keep on regularly and rapidly changing, the market is volatile.

Volatility can affect option pricing significantly. Many beginning options traders tend to ignore the implications, which can lead to huge investment losses.

Historical Volatility

Historical or statistical volatility is used to measure the changes in the price of the underlying option, so it's based on actual and real data. Let's refer to it as HV for the rest of the time. HV shows how fast the stock price has moved. The higher HV is, the more the stock price has moved during a certain period. So, when a stock has a high HV, the price is more likely to move, at least theoretically. It's more of a future movement indication and not a real guarantee.

On the other hand, a low HV might indicate the stock price hasn't moved much, but it might be going in one direction steadily. You can use HV to predict somewhat how much a security's price will change based on how fast it changed in the past, but you can't use it to predict an actual trend.

HV is measured over a certain period, such as a week, month, or year and you can compute for it in various ways.

Implied Volatility

Another type of volatility that options traders should be aware of is Implied Volatility or IV. Whereas HV measures a security's past volatility, IV is more of an estimate of its future volatility.

IV is a projection of how fast and how much the stock price is likely to change in price. Many beginning traders focus on the profitability (difference in strike price and stock price) and the contract expiration when considering an option's price, but IV also plays a major role.

You can determine option IV by considering factors such as the stock and strike prices, length of time before expiration, current interest rate, and HV. Since IV in an option may indicate how much the stock will change in price, the price increases when the IV itself increases. Because theoretically, more profit can be gained when there are dramatic movements in the price of the underlying stock. An option's price can also change significantly even when the stock price remains the same, usually caused by its IV.

For example, ABC is about to release a new product and speculations build-up that the company is about to announce it. The options IV for stock ABC can be very high since there are expectations of significant movement in the underlying stock price. The announcement might be received well, and the stock price might go up, or the audience will be disappointed with the new product, and stock prices drop quickly. In this scenario, the stock price might not significantly move since investors will be waiting for the press release before buying or selling stocks. The extrinsic value will then be increased for both puts and calls rather than the stock price movement. It is one way that IV can affect option pricing.

If you're betting that a stock's price will dramatically increase once that announcement has been made, you may purchase "at-the-money" Call options to maximize probable gains for that increase. If ABC announced and was well received, causing the stock prices to shoot up, there would have been significant gains in the Call options' intrinsic value. After the press release and the stock price movement, IV will be lower since it's predicted that the stock price won't change very soon. There will then be a substantial fall on the calls' extrinsic value, which would offset most of the profit you gained with the increased intrinsic value.

Volatility Skew

Different implied volatility percentages at different strike prices will give rise to trading opportunities. If you show the implied volatility percentage next to each strike price in the option chain, you can see a different percentage at each strike price, even though it is the same underlying instrument. If you were to graph the different percentages as you move up and down the option chain, you would see a pattern that is called a "skew." The trading platform should allow you to view the implied volatility percentage next to each strike price.

A forward bias happens when the percentage of implied volatility rises when you move higher at the strike price (i.e., at-the-money implied volatility is 25%, and the higher strike price is 32%). A reverse skew trend occurs as the percentage of implied volatility decreases when you move higher at the strike price (i.e., at-the-money implied volatility is 25%, and the higher strike price is 22 percent). A smiling skew occurs when the implied volatility percentage rises when you move both higher and lower away from the at-the-money strike price (i.e., at-the-money implied volatility is 25% and equidistant higher and lower strike prices are 32%). A flat skew occurs when the implied volatility percentage stays relatively stable whether you shift lower or higher in the strike price (i.e., at-the-money implied volatility is 25 percent, and higher and lower strike prices are close to 25 percent).

Can you guess which skew pattern reflects the typical stock graphically? The correct answer is the reverse skew, so that's where you need to concentrate your attention. For some agricultural futures, a forward skew may be popular.

A reverse skew pattern occurs when the percentage of implied volatility decreases when you increase the strike price. It means that call implied volatility percentages decrease as you move out-of-the-money further (to higher strike prices and increase implied volatility percentages as you move out-of-money further to lower strike prices). The skew will help you decide the out-of-the-money choices are right for you to buy and sell. For example, assuming that all other variables are the same, you can sell an option with a higher implied volatility percentage and buy an option with a lower implied volatility percentage, thereby providing a theoretical volatility edge.

Asymmetrical slant/bias in the value of call versus call can affect your trading strategy. For example, if a call's value is greater than that of a put, you can exchange a collar more easily, where a call is sold, and the proceeds are used to buy a put. The implied volatility percentage pattern can vary from Call to Put, even if it is for the same underlying stock (or futures).

Calendar Volatility Skew

Volatility skews can still occur if you step further out in time, even if the strike price is the same. It is common for a near-term (first month) on-the-money option to have more implied volatility than a longer-term option for equity options. For example, assume that XYZ is trading $100 a share in January. The February 100 Call option maybe $5 ($500) with an implied volatility rate of 60 percent, and the March 100 Call option maybe $7 ($700) with an implied volatility rate of 50 percent.

CHAPTER 24:

Iron Condor

The Logic Behind the Iron Condor

The Iron Condor combines a Put Credit Spread and a Call Credit Spread into a single trade. I know, it sounds extremely complicated. Now we are talking about four options in a single trade. But the truth is that it's not that complicated.

So, to set this up, you estimate what the range of the stock is. You want to look over a reasonable time and then determine the lowest share price the stock will hit. It doesn't predict what will happen in the future, but it does give us a boundary point that we can use. It is all about playing the probability game. So, we estimate the probability that the stock will stay within some range of values.

Now we do the same for the upper bound. If a stock price doesn't change very much, it will be ranging between these two values without having any breakout.

It is the secret of the success of the Iron Condor. The first step to set it up is to sell a Call option at a higher boundary price. Then, we sell a Put option at the lower boundary price.

Selling these two options gives us a net credit. The Iron Condor is another limited risk strategy, though. To minimize the risk, we are going to buy two options that lie on the outside range. You will buy a Put option with a lower strike price than the Put option that we sold. You can see now that we have set up a Put Credit Spread.

Next, we buy a Call option with a higher strike price than the Call option that we sold. So, this sets up a Call Credit Spread. But when you combine the two into a single trade, you set up an interior boundary for the stock to move around in.

Suppose that a stock is trading at $100 a share. We could sell a Call option with a strike price of $105. Then we could sell a Put option with a strike price of $95. It sets up our zone of profitability. As long as the stock stays within the range of $95 to $105 per share until option expiration, we are in a profitable situation. To mitigate the risk, we buy two options with outside strike prices. So, we could go with a Call option with a strike price of $110 and then buy a Put option with a strike price of $90.

The strategy on these is to wait and hope the stock price doesn't break out. If it doesn't, you can let the options expire, and you will earn a profit from the net credit you have received. The net credit is going to be given by this:

Credit received selling high strike put + credit received selling low strike call – debit paid for high strike price call – debit paid for low strike price put.

There is some argument about whether or not you buy or sell an Iron Condor, but people arguing about this are just confused. You are selling an Iron Condor. It is because you are selling to open, and you receive a net credit for the trade.

If things go bad, that is, the stock does have a breakout one way or another, you will have losses, but they will be capped. If it's not working out, you can always buy back the Iron Condor to close the position. As with other trades, if you are risk-averse and worried about something amazing happening with the stock on expiration day, you can always buy back the Iron Condor to close the position early. However, remember that this move will cut down on your profits, limited already by the credit received for entering the position.

When to Use an Iron Condor

You want to use an Iron Condor when a stock is not expected to move very much. Some people pick options with very low Delta values, like 0.16, so they are far outside the money. It can give the stock a wider range of values to oscillate around in, but you will make smaller profits per option contract. That said, it increases the probability of earning a profit. So once again, we have a trade-off.

You will not want to put an Iron Condor on when the stock has a high amount of implied volatility. High implied volatility will mean that there is a higher probability that the stock will move outside one of the boundaries that you have setup with the Iron Condor.

One situation that definitely would not be used with an Iron Condor is before an earnings Call. You do not want to have an Iron Condor in stock before the earnings Call. If the stock rises to a new range, it might be possible to use an Iron Condor to earn income off the stock after settling down.

You might choose low volatility stocks for Iron Condors. For example, a relatively stable stock like IBM (outside of earnings season) could be a possible choice. But like any options trade, you will want to see what the open interest is on the options you are considering for your Iron Condor.

Why Use an Iron Condor

Traders use Iron Condors because it's a limited risk strategy that can be used to generate regular income from trading. Selling an Iron Condor is analogous to selling a Put Credit Spread in that you are going to need a certain amount of collateral to cover the trade. So, while the Iron Condor is in your account, the money you use to cover it will be tied up until you close the position or you let the options expire, assuming that you don't incur losses because the share price remains in the range that you've set up for the trade.

Let's consider a real-world example. It will show that unlike the spreads that we considered, an Iron Condor has losses on the upside and the downside, with a range of profitability in between. The losses are not necessarily equal. In this example, we consider an Iron Condor on Facebook with strike prices of $192.50 and $212.50. It is quite a wide range; it's wide enough that it might survive the upcoming earnings call. Maximum losses occur when the share price goes above the high strike price call or below the low strike price put. In this example, the high strike price call is $215. The low strike price put is $187.50.

On the upside, if the share price rises above $215, there is a maximum loss of $55.

On the downside, if the share price goes below $187.50, the maximum loss is $305. The collateral required is always the larger of the two potential losses, so to enter into this trade, you'd have to deposit $305 into your account.

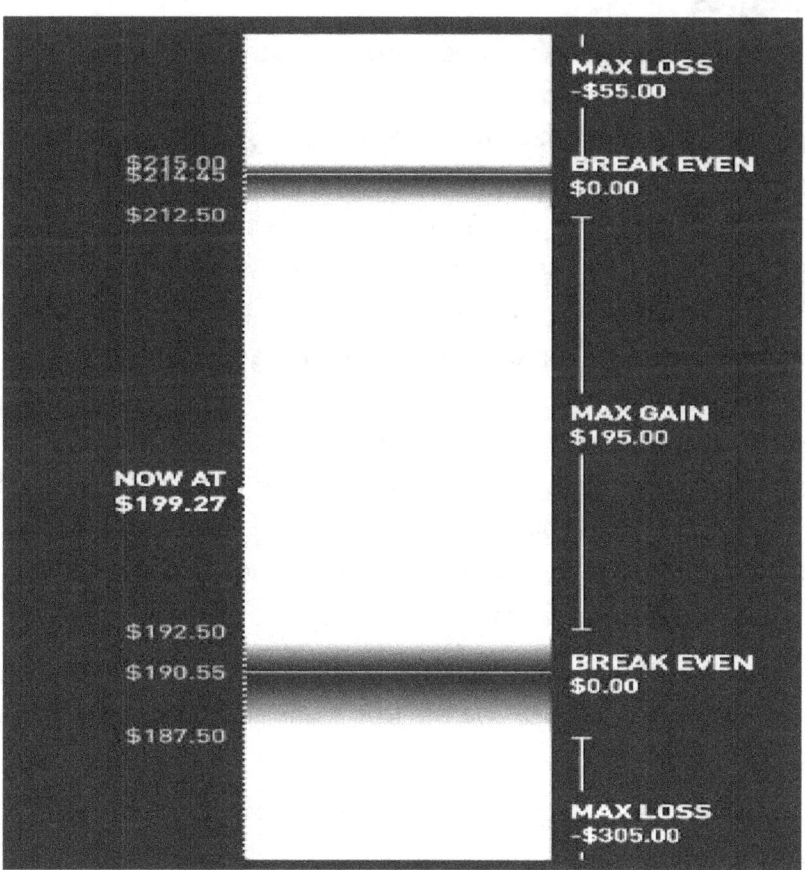

You can see that if the share price stays in between the inner strike prices, the maximum profit of $195 (the credit received for selling to open the position) is realized.

The assignment's risk is the same as for a Put Credit Spread or Call Credit Spread—it's not something you have to worry about. If an assignment occurs, the broker is all handled automatically, and the stocks will be quickly bought and sold without you even noticing.

So, the credit received on a per-share basis is $1.95. The upper put strike price gives the break-even point on the downside minus the credit received, $192.50 - $1.95 = $190.55. The lower call strike price gives the upper break-even point plus the credit received, so in this case, that would be $212.50 + $1.95 = $214.45.

For the strike prices, you choose out-of-the-money values. An Iron Condor is considered a non-directional strategy. You only care that the share price stays within a given range of values—you don't care if it goes up or goes down within that range.

Options Strategies

There are many choices available to options traders to either profit from stock moves or earn income. Different strategies are used in different situations. If you want to become a successful options trader, you need to memorize which trades are used in which situation.

Some traders specialize in only doing one or two types of trades. So, for example, a trader might only go along with calls and puts. That is a simple strategy that is easy to understand, but there is also the highest risk of entering a losing trade when following that type of strategy.

Many traders only trade for income. These types of traders who are level 3 and below will only use Iron Condor, Put Credit Spread, Call Credit Spread, covered calls, or protected puts, among the strategies.

However, among those, traders tend to specialize. So, there are traders who will do nothing but Iron Condors, while other traders will do nothing but Put Credit Spreads. This approach can have its advantages because you will become an expert on one type of trade. When you become an expert on one type of trade, you will have a higher probability of success.

Let's give a summary of the types of trades for different situations.

- Non-directional trade but stock not moving much. Used for a stock expected to range between two values. Use the Iron Condor. Stock is not expected to move by a large amount.

- Stock will move by a large amount in a non-directional trade. Use Strangles and Straddles.

- You think a stock will go up, and you want maximum profits. Buy a Call option.

- You think a stock will go up, but you want to limit risk and are willing to limit profits to cut risk. Buy a Call Debit Spread.

- You think a stock will go down, and you want maximum profits. Buy a Put option.

- You think a stock will go down, but you want to limit risk and will trade limited profits for your protection. Buy a Put Debit Spread.

- You want to earn income but think the stock will go up or stay about the same. Sell a Put Credit Spread.

- You want to earn income but think the stock will go down or stay about the same. Sell a Call Credit Spread.

- You own shares of stock and want to earn money against them. Sell Covered Calls.

- You have cash on hand and want to earn money without buying stock. Sell Protected Puts against the cash.

CHAPTER 25:

Money Management

Your mindset provides you with a strong opportunity to hedge yourself against risk in your trades, but it is not the only way to protect yourself. You also need to make sure that you are protecting yourself in practical ways against risks in the market to take advantage of all of the tools available to help you succeed.

When it comes to trading, you can never be too careful, and you should always be exercising every technique possible to protect yourself against risks in the market.

Protecting Through Diversifying

One of the best things you can do to protect yourself when you are trading is diversifying your portfolio. Diversifying your portfolio means investing your capital into multiple different trade deals to invest in several different areas. The reason why diversification hedges you against risk is that it prevents you from the likelihood of total losses.

In this case, if one of your trades does not perform well, another one of your trades is likely to outperform it and make up for that loss. As long as you are doing your best to research every single trade and trade with confidence, you are likely to see success in many of your trades if you use this strategy, and the losses you do see will not be nearly as catastrophic.

Conclusion

Options trading involves a selection of considerations both before as well as after the trade has been placed. Many of the mistakes mentioned may be accounted for before the trade is opened using the tools and materials. The one most significant step to trading options is developing a scheme as well as stick with it! Here you find tools that will help you build your plan. Take advantage of these and other trading resources to allow you to stay away from typical mistaken choices in trading in your future trades.

Once again, options trading is not for everybody. However, based upon hard-won, individual experience, it provides you with the details you require to see if options trading is an excellent individual chance for you on your journey to monetary liberty and security.

This guide offers you the type of standard details you've been trying to find to make an educated choice about options trading. Make no mistake about it; this kind of speculative stock trading is not for everybody. By setting out the procedure you require to go through in a practical and useful method, you get a clear concept of precisely what you'll be entering when you begin your options trading.

Far from dissuading or downhearted, it also provides a practical and well-balanced view of what it's like to prepare to trade, in addition to the truths you'll deal with when you day trade. You get vital pointers on the state of mind you require to embrace, the tools you need to get, crucial strategies that are effective and reliable to option traders, and directions on establishing your extremely own effective options trading individual method.

You are looking at the ideal book if you are a total rookie to options trading and desire to start operating in this field. Rather than investing an excessive quantity of words on how much you can make from options trading, this book focuses most of its firepower on what you require to understand to succeed with options trading.

One of my favorite things about options is that you can get involved in options trading without having a lot of money. If people were smart and disciplined about it, options trading could even provide a way out of a low-income situation. You can start trading with a hundred dollars, and if you are careful with it a year from now, you could significantly grow that into a large trading account.

Just remember that options trading is a serious business, but it can be fun and exciting too. There is no reason why making money has to be tedious and difficult. You can get involved at the highest levels of our economy with the best companies by trading options. You will be able to go by on the stock market and earn some of your profits. Good start!